How Real Is
Your God?

HOW REAL IS YOUR GOD?

THE DEATH AND LIFE OF JONATHAN LEBER

KATHY LEBER

Pleasant Word

Pleasant Word (a division of WinePress Publishing, PO Box 428, Enumclaw, WA 98022) functions only as book publisher. As such, the ultimate design, content, editorial accuracy, and views expressed or implied in this work are those of the author.

Unless otherwise noted, all Scriptures are taken from the King James Version of the Bible.

ISBN 1-4141-0795-1
Library of Congress Catalog Card Number: 2006906278

In Memorium

The Jonathan Leber Preacher Boy Scholarship
at
Fairfax Baptist Temple Academy has been established
to support young men or women who
enroll in a fundamental Bible college to
prepare for full-time Christian service.
Donations may be sent to:
Fairfax Baptist Temple
6401 Missionary Lane
Fairfax Station, VA 22039

The Jonathan Leber Memorial Scholarship
at
Maranatha Baptist Bible College
has been established to support students majoring in
Missions or Missions Aviation.
Donations may be sent to:
Maranatha Baptist Bible College
745 W. Main Street,
Watertown, WS 53094

TABLE OF CONTENTS

Foreword

How real is your God? That's an interesting question, and it is certainly a question that deserves an answer. However, as you read the story of the life of Jon Leber the question that you will be compelled to answer is, how real are you before the one True God of the Universe?

In September 1991, Fairfax Baptist Temple received John, Kathy, and Jonathan Leber into its membership. (Upon young Danielle's salvation two years later she joined with the church subsequent to her baptism.) Jon was just a week shy of turning eight years old when his family started attending FBT. My strongest memories of Jon as a young boy are that he was a happy child and always quick to offer an exuberant, "Hello, Pastor."

Through the pages of this book, in the words of the various sermons that he had written, you will find that Jon was a young man working at developing his understanding of how God has defined Himself in the words of Scripture. You will see a young man growing in his understanding, coming to grips with the reality that having a relationship with God the Father comes only through salvation by the grace of God through personal faith in Jesus Christ. Jon was in the process of discovering as well that with salvation comes a responsibility to find and do the work that God has before ordained for every believer.

Whatever the specific work that God has ordained for you happens to be, you will discover, as Jon was discovering, that the work involves soul-winning. God the Father sent His Son to seek and to save the lost. Jesus Christ sent His first disciples to accomplish the same work. His commission for the church is the same-carry on the task of winning souls until the moment that in the twinkling of an eye, we are called home.

God summoned Jon to Himself much earlier in Jon's life than any of us would have imagined. I'm forced to observe that each of us must live for God fully and completely every day because none of us knows when we will be similarly summoned.

Is God real to you? Are you living your life as though God is real? I know that anyone reading this book, whether young or old, will be challenged to take a look deep inside to be sure that as the last breath is drawn—whenever and under whatever circumstance—that there will be no shame as the glorious face of the Savior comes into a focus sharper than any image here on earth.

Dr. Bud Calvert.
Pastor Emeritus,
Fairfax Baptist Temple.

ACKNOWLEDGEMENTS

Next to enjoyment of the love of God and as-surance of a home in heaven, the best thing about being a Christian is sharing the warmth and friendship of a lot of wonderful people. If there's ever a time to learn the real meaning and value of Christian fellowship, it's when some trial or disaster suddenly backs you against the wall. Through the tragic circumstances of the death of our beloved son we have experienced first-hand what it means to be loved and supported and sustained by the prayers and practical help of a large and vibrant Christian "family".

There are so many to thank. This book is a tangible way to express our gratitude. In addition, we want to acknowledge some individuals whose impact on Jonathan's life, and ours, has been especially significant, and some whose support in the turbulent days immediately following the events of April 25, 2005 was especially helpful. Many of Jonathan's friends, and ours, are located across the United States and across the world, in New Zealand, Australia, and Europe.

First on our recognition list is Danielle, our daughter and Jonathan's younger sister, who shared so intensely in our pain yet maintained her focus, her patience and sound advice. Her grandfather Daniel Leber also merits special recognition for coming each day to our home during the first week after Jonathan's death, just to be there for us, and who has been a constant source of comfort.

Beyond our immediate family we think of Lori and Scott Silsbee, missionaries to New Zealand, who so generously enabled Jonathan to see first-hand life on the mission field and played such a key role in his surrender to God's will.

Pastor Bud Calvert (now Pastor Emeritus of Fairfax Baptist Temple) was our spiritual shepherd during most of Jonathan's growing up years. He led the memorial service at our church and was such an encouragement to our family as we grieved over the loss of our son.

Thanks also to the many Fairfax Baptist Temple members who gave so graciously to a Scholarship Memorial Fund in memory of Jonathan and who daily prayed for us and provided many words and cards of encouragement. Thanks to many of Jonathan's classmates, friends, and teachers from Fairfax

Baptist Temple Academy who shared with us their thoughts and memories of our son-especially Jason LeGrand, Anthony Mandela, Haley Ruffner, Amanda Darby (Probus), Matthew Hawes, Sami Gaber, Walter Fedrowitz, Satish Chacko, Nadine Stillwell, Mrs. Sandy Kester, Mrs. Amy Lampert, Mrs. Sarah Pigott, Mrs. Diane Groover, Mr. and Mrs. Dewey Carr, Mr. and Mrs. Gil Hansen, Mr. and Mrs. Mark Winslow, and Tip Tatusko.

Thanks to the many college professors, college friends, and college classmates who shared their experiences with Jonathan: among them are Eric A. Hafeli, Sr., Tim Zajicek, Shamar Bailey, Dale and Jessica Mundt, Matty Ledgerwood, Emily Zielke, and Aaron Lewber. Thanks to Dr. Dave Jasper for leading a college that trains and prepares young men and women for a life of full-time service in the work of the Lord, and for hosting a memorial service for Jonathan.

Thanks to Mark Cruse (coach of Watertown High School Swim Team), Billy Buchholtz, Thuy and Alaina McMurray, and Amy Baillargeon for their thoughts, support, and kind words. Thanks to Diane Fortune and Mrs. LaSalle who continue to check on us and give us words of comfort.

Thanks to the Coast Guard who searched for Jonathan immediately after he went into Lake Michigan, and to the divers from Pirate's Cove Dive Company (Jerry Guyer and Bob Schaefer) who retrieved his belongings from the airplane, his cell phone and ultimately the airplane itself from Lake Michigan.

To Rob Van den Berg, thanks for helping us to decipher the pilot and control tower dialog from tapes we received.

Thanks to Edward Thal for his many hours of editing and finalizing this book to prepare it for publication.

And heartfelt thanks to all of the wonderful people who are unnamed but were instrumental in providing graceful encouragement and warm Christian love during our time of trial-many of whom continue to pray for us.

Most of all, we thank God for allowing us to share how He can be real in one's life, even in the midst of uncertainty and turmoil. From the start, God molded Jonathan's life and above all He should be praised.

John and Kathy Leber.
Fairfax, Virginia.
July, 2006.

INTRODUCTION

I got to know Jonathan Leber more through his death than in his life. The interest in him that sprang from the unusual circumstances of his death brought him sharply into focus for many people and his story took on a dimension that was almost larger than life. I met him briefly, once, and heard him preach once, but the greater details of who he was and what he did and what he planned to do would have gone largely unobserved by me and others like me, on the periphery of his life, were it not for the fact that his plane fell into Lake Michigan on a cold winter's night and he disappeared without a trace.

Several things impressed me from the telling of his story.

The first is the glory and triumph of Christianity itself. It is remarkable how many people including

Jonathan's parents speak with confidence and anticipation about meeting him again and renewing their relationships with him. These comments are made not with bravado or from any sense of desperation: they are simple statements of fact. To friends and family alike, Jonathan is not lost—he is just assigned elsewhere in God's domain and the separation is only temporary.

Then there is the identity of Jonathan himself: just how superhuman was this 20-year-old? The answer of course is that he was a fallible, sinful young man who was inspired by Jesus Christ to launch out on a grand enterprise that made his successes more worthwhile and diminished his failures. Measured by the yardstick of contemporary society and culture he was ordinary, if perhaps a little strange in the direction of his passions away from the things of this world. Yet that very "strangeness" added an extraordinary dimension to his life.

Lastly, there is the identity of Jonathan's family and friends. To say that they are diverse would be an understatement, yet they were all linked in some way to him and to each other, or were affected in some way by him, through his relationship with Jesus Christ. His was not a dead religion but a living relationship with a living Savior and this was no more evident than in his relationships with others.

It has been a pleasure to get to know him through the pages of this book.

—Edward Thal.

A Preacher At His Own Funeral

The church was crowded that Spring Wednesday in 2005. There was an expectant hush as the young man paused for a moment, scanning the crowd, then leaned forward slightly and posed a question: "How real is your God?"

The challenge hung in the air as he announced his text, Hebrews 11:6:

> *Without faith it is impossible to please Him: for he that cometh to God must believe that He is, and that He is a rewarder of them that diligently seek Him.*

Jonathan Leber was about to preach his own funeral. A funeral without a casket. His body lay somewhere in the dark and icy waters of Lake Michigan, but his spirit was alive that day in the hearts and memories of his family and friends as we heard again the familiar words he had preached from that very spot just a few months before. Now he spoke, larger than life, from a video that had been recorded on that day.

His words had an almost prophetic ring to them.

How real is your God? Not only is our faith important to our belief in God, but it is and should be our most prized and most valuable possession. I Peter 1:7 reads:

> *That the trial of your faith, being much more precious than of gold that perisheth, though it be tried with fire, might be found unto praise and honour and glory at the appearing of Jesus Christ.*

This past semester at Maranatha Baptist Bible College, we had our annual Missions Conference. However, we were blessed with a special speaker that I personally knew, Pastor Bob McLain. During that week, Pastor McLain and I had lunch together and began some small talk. He started asking me about my dating/love life, jobs, and my future in the ministry. I responded to his questions, especially the latter with answers that he saw as pretty well thought-out plans.

But then he asked me what God had planned for my life! I was speechless. I knew that God had plans for my future but I did not really know specifically where I would be. Whether after I graduated, I would get my Masters or become an intern at a church or go on deputation. I just didn't know. Pastor McLain noticed my hesitation and responded in his soft tone, 'Jonathan Leber, how real is your God?'

When he asked me that question, something clicked and I realized that I had been living my college career up to that point for myself and I was not taking that step of faith that I needed to. I was not relying on God for my present activities or my future plans. Today, we will look at four men of God that took that step of faith and found out how real their God was to each of them.

First, let us look at Noah and how he demonstrated his faith in God. The passage in Genesis 6:5 through 12, reads:

> And God saw that the wickedness of man was great in the earth, and that every imagination of the thoughts of his heart was only evil continually.
> And it repented the LORD that He had made man on the earth, and it grieved him at his heart.
> And the LORD said, I will destroy man whom I have created from the face of the earth; both man, and beast, and the creeping thing, and the fowls of the air; for it repenteth Me that I have made them.
> But Noah found grace in the eyes of the LORD.
> These are the generations of Noah: Noah was a just man and perfect in his generations, and Noah walked with God.
> And Noah begat three sons, Shem, Ham, and Japheth.
> The earth also was corrupt before God, and the earth was filled with violence.

And God looked upon the earth, and behold, it was corrupt; for all flesh had corrupted his way upon the earth.'

As seen in this passage, the wickedness of man has caused God to want to destroy the evil by destroying mankind. God found one man that pleased Him and because of his faith, God would save him and his family. Noah and his family also had to take another step of faith in order to be saved from the flood. They would have to build an ark to the exact blueprints that God gave them, even though they were not near any large body of water. God later rewarded them for their faith. How real is your God? Hebrews 11:7 states:

By faith Noah, being warned of God of things not seen as yet, moved with fear, prepared an ark to the saving of his house; by the which he condemned the world, and became heir of the righteousness which is by faith.

Secondly, let us look at Abraham's life and his faith in God. Genesis 12:1 through 4 reads:

Now the Lord had said unto Abram, Get thee out of thy country, and from thy kindred, and from thy father's house, unto a land that I will show thee: And I will make of thee a great nation, and I will bless thee, and make thy name great; and thou shalt be a blessing: And I will bless them that bless thee, and curse him that curseth thee: and in thee shall all families of the earth be blessed.

So Abram departed, as the Lord had spoken unto him; and Lot went with him: and Abram was seventy and five years old when he departed out of Haran.

As seen through Abraham's life, God told Abraham to leave his homeland and his relatives and to go to a place where God wanted him. And Abraham obeyed God through faith and left everything that he had grown up with to go to some far off distant land as a servant of God. How real is your God? Hebrews 11:8 reads:

By faith Abraham, when he was called to go out into a place which he should after receive for an inheritance, obeyed; and he went out, not knowing whither he went.

Thirdly, we have Job's example of faith. In Job 1:20 through 22, the passage reads:

Then Job arose, and rent his mantle, and shaved his head, and fell down upon the ground, and worshipped, and said, Naked came I out of my mother's womb, and naked shall I return thither: the Lord gave, and the Lord hath taken away, blessed be the name of the Lord.
In all this Job sinned not, nor charged God foolishly.

Satan failed to make Job sin! Instead of cursing God, Job worshipped God. He had lost two of his most precious possessions: his family and his wealth. Yet he remained upright and steadfast in his faith in

God. Satan went on to test Job by giving him boils, and on top of that his friends and even his wife told him to curse God and die, but Job remained faithful to God throughout this trial and God blessed him with double of everything he had. The Bible reads in Job 42:10:

> *And the Lord turned the captivity of Job, when he prayed for his friends: also the Lord gave Job twice as much as he had before.*

How real is your God?

The fourth example was Daniel and his faith in God even as an evil plan is devised. Darius the Mede sets about to reorganize and consolidate his new kingdom, Babylon. He divides the kingdom into provinces with governors. These governors are accountable to three presidents and Daniel is one of these presidents. Although Daniel was over eighty years old, he was blessed with so much skill and abilities that Darius considered elevating him over the other two presidents. As a result, the other two presidents were angered and they plotted to have Daniel's life taken. Since these two presidents were unable to find a flaw in his secular life, they decided to trap him in his religious life. They tricked King Darius into signing a 30 day decree which said that all praying during that time must be directed to the king himself. When Daniel learned of this decree, he was determined more than ever to not compromise his belief in God but to show the world that God is real and in control of every situation even if it may look hopeless to the world and their standards. Daniel 6:10 and 11 reads:

> *Now when Daniel knew that the writing was signed, he went into his house; and his windows being open in his chamber toward Jerusalem, he kneeled upon his knees three times a day, and prayed, and gave thanks before his God, as he did aforetime.*
> *Then these men assembled, and found Daniel praying and making supplication before His God.*

They immediately rushed to Darius and told him that Daniel disobeyed the decree. Daniel was arrested and thrown down into a den of hungry lions. After the den is sealed with the signet ring, Darius spends a sleepless night in the palace. The next morning, the king rushes to the den and discovers that Daniel is still alive. As a result, Darius took vengeance upon the men who tricked him in the first place and had those men along with families thrown into the lion's den and the lions instantly ate the people.

Even though the law had been written that no one could pray or worship anyone or any God but King Darius, Daniel still prayed and worshipped God (The One True and Only Real God), because he knew that his God would take care of him. His faith in God kept him serving God even when he was threatened with death. We are not even threatened by death to serve God, but we struggle with passing out tracts, talking about God and our faith, and sadly we sometimes struggle with going to church. How real is your God?

During the summer, one of my many jobs is instructing water aerobics. At the end of the summer before my freshman year of college, one of the older ladies in my class gave me a card thanking me for a great summer. This card also contained this silver dollar. In the card she wrote, 'Jonathan, as you go to college and you continue to go on life's journey, keep this coin with you to remind you to stay strong in your faith and trust in God. Just as the founding fathers of our great nation put their trust in God and made our motto 'In God We Trust.'

After seeing the examples of these everyday simple men of the Old Testament that were used of God to do great things, because they knew how real their God was, we need to take a minute and ask ourselves, How real is my God? Is He real enough for me to witness to my co-worker, my neighbor, or my relatives? Is my God real enough for me to hand the clerk at a grocery store a tract or maybe a waiter or even someone on the street? Is my God real enough for me to leave the comforts of my home or even my job to go to some little rural town in the middle of nowhere to be a pastor of some small country church, or even leave the comforts of my homeland to serve other people in some far off country?

How real is your God? Today, is the day to decide!
Our talents and our possessions
We dare not ever hoard
But share them with real gratitude
As unto Christ our Lord.
Faith honors God...God honors faith!

Jesus stated in Matthew 17:20:

If ye have faith as a grain of mustard seed, ye shall say unto this mountain, Remove hence to yonder place; and it shall remove; and nothing shall be impossible unto you.

The question remains: How real is your God?

CHAPTER TWO

MAYDAY!

Milwaukee approach, I'm...I'm running out of fuel right now."

The young man's voice was calm but tense, with a slightly metallic ring to it from the recording device. He had been talking to the Milwaukee control tower for several minutes during his approach across Lake Michigan. The call sign of his small Piper Archer aircraft was November 60 Foxtrot.

"Okay November 60 Fox are you declaring an emergency?"

"Ah, yes, sir."

"Okay, I'm going to turn the lights up for all the runways here and I want you to report Milwaukee in sight. Right now it is at your 12 o'clock and one two miles.".

"Okay, I see it."

"I'm going to give you any runway you want and just let me know which one you want? Northwest 10-26 turn right into 170 and intercept localizer"

"170 intercept the localizer Northwest 10-26"

"Okay, November 60 Fox I understand you do have the airport in sight and, ah, like I said, I can give you any runway you want. The wind is now 230 at 11."

"Ah, I got that. Yeah, my, ah, my one tank went out so I have like a quarter, ah three gallons left... Tower Northwest 10-26? Northwest 10-26 cleared to land?"

"Okay clear to land Northwest 10-26"

"Milwaukee approach...60 Fox...land."

"November 60 Fox, you're breaking up. Do you have the airport?"

"No, I'm...I'm still out...out in the..."

"Okay, November 60 Fox, you're breaking up. I'm going to turn up all runway lights right now for you...November 60 Fox if you could, turn on your landing lights please?"

"The landings lights are on but I'm in the clouds."

"Oh Okay!...November 60 Fox about maybe 3 miles west of your position there should be breaks in the, ah, in the lower layer right now."

"I...I have the land in sight but I don't think I can glide that far."

"November 60 Fox you said you don't think you have enough to get this far?"

"I don't."

"Okay, I'm alerting emergency air, emergency numbers at this time."

"I'm like 5 feet off the water, Milwaukee. I'm like 5 feet off the water!"

The Milwaukee control tower tries to direct an air ambulance flying in the vicinity towards the stricken plane.

"Medics 812 maintain 3,000 and I'm going to turn you to zero niner zero, the last known position of this aircraft. To maintain 3,000 zero niner zero Medics 812."

"You want us zero niner zero right now Medics 812?"

"Yes, sir please!"

"Right to zero niner zero Medics 812. Did you get that call from him?"

"No I did not Medics 812.

"He said Mayday, Mayday, Mayday!"

"Medics 812, thanks a lot, I'm not getting it at all."

"He just trying to contact you. He said he's in the water…You sitting on the airplane?…He wants to know if he should get out of the airplane?"

"Does he have a flotation device?"

"Do you have a flotation device?"

"Does he have emergency gear?"

"Do you have any flotation device or emergency gear? Flares especially?… Maybe a life jacket? Life jacket or anything?…And how many people please? How many people do you have on board?"

"Ah…Medics turn right heading 180. The last known report was right where you're at right now about to your right and about 2 miles."

"Okay, if we could get lower, we might be able to get under the, ah, under the overcast here."

"Medics 812 maintain 2,500, I think that's as low as I can give you right now."

"2,500 Medics 812."

Then, amazingly, a telephone call comes through to 911.

"Milwaukee Sheriff 911 mobile, this is Mark. How may I help you?"

"Yea, I ditched my plane, just ran out of fuel on me. I'm 5 miles off of Timmerman and I need, I need help really fast."

"Okay, What are you, what are you doing sir?"

"I'm sitting on my plane right now."

"Okay, are you flying or are you on the ground?"

"I'm on, I'm in Michigan, in Lake Michigan."

"You're in Michigan?"

"Yeah, my plane ran out of fuel."

"Okay, you're in the air or on the ground?"

"No, I'm in the water!"

"Okay, do you know where in Michigan?"

"About 5 miles east of Timmerman, ah, not Tim-merman, Milwaukee Airport."

"Okay, you're in the lake?"

"Yeah!"

"Okay, stay on the line with me and I'm going to transfer you right to the airport, okay?"

"I…I…I have about three minutes left before…"

"Okay, you're 5 miles east of the airport in the lake."

"Yes."

"Okay, what type of plane do you have?"

"A Piper Archer."

"Piper Archer?"

"Yes! The airport knows but, ah…"

"What's your first name?"

"The airport knows my plane's going down fast!"

"Okay, what's your first name?"

"Jonathan Leber."

"Do you have flotation equipment, Jonathan?"

"No, I don't."

"Do you know how to swim?"

"Yes!"

"Okay, what's your cell phone number?"

"703 625-1869."

"625-1829?..69…1869?"

"I'm in the water."

"Jonathan? Jonathan?"

"Help!"

"Jonathan?"

"Yeah…"

As his voice trailed off, the sound of water, and then a click, marked the sudden end of the call. Jonathan began the swim of his life in the freezing waters of Lake Michigan.

Medical experts described what it must have been like in those final moments. The cold water was an iron bar hitting him in the forehead and jerking his head back as the waves came toward him. Icy needles pierced his entire face. It felt as if he had put his face straight into the freezer and shut the door. His upper lip quickly went numb, like the effect of an anesthetic at the dentist. His teeth were on edge, as if he'd been eating ice cream all day long. It became harder and harder to maintain a steady rhythm of strokes through the water as his rapidly cooling body drew blood from his extremities to support his vital organs. Hands, feet, then arms and legs lost all feeling. He would continue swimming until hypothermia overcame him and all movement ceased.

CHAPTER THREE

A Good Day For Flying

The last day of Jonathan Leber's life began well. He was passionate about flying and today he would be going cross country back to Maranatha Baptist Bible College after a weekend visit to Hamilton, New York, with his friend Kyle Stuart. Jonathan would often fly for pleasure and to clock more cross country hours. On this occasion much of the return trip would be at night, giving him valuable hours of flying by instruments only.

The previous day—April 24, 2005, a Sunday—he called us at our home in Springfield, Virginia. It was about 1:00 P.M. and his father and I had just returned home from the morning service at Fairfax Baptist Temple. Jonathan told us he had landed at Niagara, New York, to top off his gas tank and the control tower would not allow him to continue his journey since the cloud ceiling was too low. We prayed for him and suggested that he should consider a hotel for the night. About midnight he called again to say that he had started to fly but within a few minutes the wings of his airplane iced up and he was forced to turn back, making an emergency landing at Niagara.

The next day, Monday, April 25th, I spoke again to Jonathan at 11:00 A.M. I told him that his sister Danielle had just finished taking her swimming pool operators test and passed with flying colors. Jonathan, a first-rate swimmer, was delighted at the news. He told me that he was still in New York, waiting for the cloud ceiling to lift. He had made a quick visit to take in the sights at Niagara Falls and was on his way back to the airport, where he arrived about noon. He stopped at the pilot's lounge to check the day's weather, then began studying for his final exams.

At last, the 12 hour forecast showed an area of low pressure approaching from the southwest. Other than some cirrus clouds and a low stratus layer, the evening looked good for flying. It was now dusk as Jonathan greeted the clerk at the front desk and headed out to the flight line to begin his preflight check. After unlocking the doors and stowing his gear, he untied the airplane, completed the preflight and hopped in as he had done many times before. He was a low-time pilot with excellent training. This was his final cross country flight before taking the instrument flight rules exam. It would be satisfying to finally have that behind him. The months prior had been filled with long hours of study and drills in precision flying by instruments alone.

Jonathan contacted ground control to let them know he was ready. He was instructed to taxi to runway 270. Everything felt good. He made it a habit to reflect on God's goodness while taxing to the assigned runway. His whole purpose in life was to serve the Lord wherever He might lead and flight preparation was to fit him for a calling in missionary aviation that might take him to a grass strip somewhere along the Amazon River, or crossing a thousand lakes in Northern Canada.

Now, preparing for takeoff, he initiated the run-up of his Piper Archer. The engine throbbed with life as he pushed the throttle to 1500 RPM. Left and right magnetos were both running normal; carburetor heard okay. Methodically working his way through the checklist, he switched to Tenth Frequency and called the tower.

"Niagara Tower, This is Piper 5360 Foxtrot ready at 270 for takeoff."

"Roger, 5360 Foxtrot. Winds are 290 at 15. Cleared for takeoff."

"Cleared for takeoff, 5360 Foxtrot," Jonathan acknowledged, pushing the throttle all the way forward as the little Piper climbed into the cold evening air. Finally she was where she belonged.

"Piper 5360, contact Niagara departure. Have a good flight!"

"Contact Niagara departure 60 Foxtrot. Thanks! Niagara departure, this is Piper 5360 Foxtrot with you through 2,500."

"Roger, 5360 Foxtrot. Radar contact 10 miles west of Niagara. Fly heading 290. Climb and maintain 6,500."

"Roger. Turn to 290, out of 2.5 for 6.5; 60 Foxtrot."

After leveling off at 6,500 feet, he prepared to cross Michigan and then Lake Michigan. He would be required to give position reports to air traffic control every 8 to10 minutes.

Since we had not heard from him that evening, I called his cell phone at 10:05 P.M. for an update. I was surprised when he answered on the first ring.

"Where are you?" I asked.

"I'm flying over Lake Huron."

I paused for a second to form a mental picture of his location, then told him, "I want you to stay focused on what you are doing. Call when you arrive. I love you!"

"I love you!" Jonathan responded. "Bye."

It was the last time we would speak to each other. I treasure that final conversation—a simple but heartfelt declaration of love between two people who understood that both our lives were bound up in an even deeper love for Jesus Christ.

Alone now in the endless night, Jonathan turned his attention to the chatter on the radio as he left Lake Huron and winged his way across Lake Michigan. The Milwaukee Control Tower was instructing another night flyer, "Right Down runway 7."

"Down runway 7 in the clear?"

Jonathan broke in: "Do you have time for a VFR?"

"Ah, what is that, the 60 Fox?"

"60 Fox, Yeah." Jonathan responded, acknowledging the call sign of his aircraft that was showing up as a little set of numbers on the Milwaukee radar. A few minutes later he called again.

"Milwaukee approach, this is 5360 Foxtrot."

"5360 Fox, Milwaukee approach Milwaukee 2niner40. What's your altitude?"

"I'm at 4,000 and…"

"Alright, November 60 Fox, I got 4,000 and you said and, and I didn't get the rest?"

"Yeah, it's 4,000, I was just looking…"

"Roger!"

Two minutes later, Jonathan radioed again: "Milwaukee approach, this is 60 Foxtrot"

"60 Fox, Milwaukee approach."

"I was wondering if I could stop at either Timmerman or Mitchell to refuel before heading on to Madison?"

"It's up to you which airport you want to refuel in."

"Ah, is Timmerman open?"

"Ah, I don't think, I don't think there's any personnel at Timmerman, I doubt it."

"Well then, I guess Mitchell…"

"Otherwise I can give you a frequency here for turn-in stand by, otherwise, ah, in the meantime expect runway 1 niner right at Milwaukee, wind ah 24013, visibility 10, ceiling 1,300 broken, 3,000 broken, 10,000 overcast up zero 2 niner 41. Unit com determines 122495 if you want to see if someone is there but I doubt it. 60 Fox did you get that?"

"Ah, yeah, 60 Fox got that."

A minute passed and Jonathan spoke up again: "Milwaukee approach 60 Foxtrot, I couldn't get anybody at Timmerman."

"Alright, then, you're landing?"

"Yes, sir."

"Alright 60 Fox plan runway, you can fly your own heading 1 niner right and report leaving 4,000"

"What was that heading?"

"I said you can fly your own heading. Do you need a vector for the airport?"

"Ah, no I can do fine."

"Just let me know if you leave 4,000. November 60 Fox did you get that?"

"Yep!"

"I would like you to acknowledge me please, it's very important. Over."

The young man who was such a careful pilot had neglected to acknowledge the air traffic control instructions because something alarming had captured his attention. About a minute later, he broke in with the flat statement that he was running out of fuel.

Jonathan had earlier reported engine trouble with the rented Piper Archer. Now, flying into 25 knot head winds across Lake Michigan he was burning up fuel and time. Suddenly, the engine cut out as the one tank ran dry and he hurriedly switched to the second tank, successfully restarting the engine. But there was very little fuel in that second tank He was in view of the airport and called the Milwaukee control tower to advise them of his predicament. A short time later he began quickly losing altitude and within minutes his tell-tale call sign disappeared off the radar screen. Jonathan had landed in Lake Michigan.

This was in itself an extraordinary demonstration of flying skill. Gliding powerless in pitch-black darkness with only his instruments to guide him, he successfully landed the single-engine airplane on top of Lake Michigan's three-foot waves, about five miles from the Wisconsin shoreline. It was 11:40 P.M. The surface water temperature was about 44 degrees with an air temperature of 32 degrees. He climbed out of the plane and sat on top of it as it settled into the frigid water. At 11:45 P.M., he dialed 911.

He had no flotation device. Though he was an excellent swimmer, the few miles to shore would prove too much for him. Coast Guard Lt. Rolando Hernandez who led a search for him until 4:00 P.M. the next day estimated that he could not have survived more than three hours in the water. The wind was blowing the choppy waves away from land and the icy air and water temperatures conspired against him.

Jonathan Leber's life—a life seemingly filled with great promise—had reached its appointed end. He was 20-years-old.

CHAPTER FOUR

THE GREATEST TRIBUTE

The memorial service for Jonathan at Fairfax Baptist Temple on May 4, 2005, was an extraordinary time of remembrance for the many hundreds of people who filled the auditorium. Besides the uncanny experience of hearing and seeing the young man speak passionately about the reality of God, there were many tributes from those who had known him best, and a reminder of the stirring words of missionary Jim Elliot, who had been martyred for his faith in an earlier generation:

He is no fool who gives what he cannot keep,
To gain what he cannot lose.

When Jonathan had gone off to college in August 2004 to continue his preparation for missionary work, he sang a solo in the same auditorium. I had written the song as a tribute to my mother, his grandmother, and now the memorial congregation heard it sung again by a friend, Amy Baillargeon:

> To be safe in the arms of Jesus,
>   Accept Him into your heart.
>   He'll be your Lord and Savior,
>   Now and forevermore.

> I'm looking and longing for loved ones,
>   Who've accepted my Lord like me.
>   I'm waiting with my Savior
>   On that bright, blissful shore.

> When my life on earth is over,
>   May I be found worthy to hear,
>   Well done thou good and faithful servant,
>   From the mouth of my Lord.

> Chorus:
>   I'm safe in the arms of Jesus,
>   Just where I want to be.
>   No more pain, sorrow or suffering,
>   But resting securely in Him.

The most fitting and lasting tribute to this young life that burned so brightly and so briefly came by way of the scores of people who were inspired by Jonathan's example. For many, the response was to surrender their lives to Jesus Christ, to share in the priceless salvation that had so transformed Jonathan. For others—those who already knew Jesus as their personal Savior—the response was to dedicate themselves to full-time Christian service.

In his death, Jonathan Leber touched more hearts than he had done even in his passionate, Christ-centered life. This, surely, is the greatest tribute of all.

CHAPTER FIVE

FOUNDATIONS

A young life that is so literally consumed by a selfless dedication to God is built not by accident but by design. It is the sum of many events, many decisions, many transforming strands that weave a pattern faithfully reflecting its foundation and structure.

Jesus Christ was Jonathan Leber's foundation. Inspiration and example from his devoted parents, from his church and school, from Christian mentors and friends, erected the structure.

His father, John and I celebrated the news of Jonathan's impending birth by turning to Psalm 127:3:

Lo, children are an heritage of the Lord,
And the fruit of the womb is His reward.

We believed then, as we believe now, that children are a priceless treasure in God's eyes. They are not a commodity. They are people that we ought to respect, and take the time to say how much we love them, then showing them how much we love them. We demonstrate our love to children by teaching them how to love the Lord.

Our desire for this child, our son, was to bring him up in the nurture and admonition of the Lord, since we saw him as a gift from God.

On September 24, 1984, at 9:08 P.M., a black haired, blue-eyed baby boy entered the world weighing 7 pounds 10 ounces. He was 21 ½ inches long. He definitely had good lungs. His cries could be heard down the corridors of Alexandria Hospital, just across the river from Washington D.C.

As I cradled my child, I recalled the second verse of the stirring hymn, "Because He Lives."

> How sweet to hold a newborn baby and feel the pride and joy he gives, But greater still the calm assurance, This child can face uncertain days, because He lives.

Jonathan was a bit of sunshine from heaven to our hearts. We loved him without reservation, yet from the very start we were determined to train him to be obedient, since a child who is obedient to his parents will find it easy to obey God.

Our resolve was soon tested. As the boy grew, so did his sin nature. He demonstrated from an early age that he had a steel will, crawling to places where he was not allowed to go or picking up things that he was told, again and again, to leave untouched. As soon as he was able to pull himself over the side of his crib, he made frequent breaks to freedom. He was a rebel, albeit a lovable one!

Over the months his hair changed color from black to red to blond. And he learned to laugh. It seemed that everything tickled him. He would laugh at a waving pillow. He would laugh at a sunbeam. He would laugh at his father's corny jokes. And he took to water like a fish. He had no fear of water. Already, the structure of his personality was becoming evident.

As he grew taller he learned more skills and habits, some good and some bad. A nightly event was his escape from his crib, diving headfirst to freedom. By the time he was two years old, the battle of wills with his parents was a full-scale war.

He wanted to be in charge. He demanded his own way. To prove his determination, he banged his head on the kitchen floor. I was first alarmed, then resolute-I would ignore him by leaving the room. As soon as he realized that he did not have an audience for his dramatic outbursts, the head-banging stopped. Over time, he began to realize that my own unyielding will was more than a match for his strength and he slowly became compliant. By the time he turned three he was a regular attender at Sunday School, church and the AWANA club-"Approved Workmen Are Not Ashamed". There, he began a lifelong habit of hiding God's Word in his heart. He was taught the letters of the alphabet and learned to associate each one with a Biblical truth.

A is for **all**. For *all* have sinned, and come short of the glory of God (Romans 3:23).

B is for **believe**. *Believe* on the name of His Son, Jesus Christ...(1 John 3:23).

C is for **Christ**....While we were yet sinners *Christ* died for us (Romans 5:8).

D is for **day**. This is the *day* which the Lord hath made; we will rejoice and be glad
in it (Psalm 118:24).

E is for **everlasting**. He that believeth on the Son hath *everlasting* life...
(John 3:36).

F is for **forgive**....The Son of Man [Jesus] hath power on earth to *forgive* sins...
(Mark 2:10).

G is for **great**....The Lord is *great*, and greatly to be praised...(Psalm 96:4).

H is for **helper**....The Lord is my *helper*...
(Hebrews 13:6).

I is for **I**....*I* [Jesus] will never leave thee [you]...
(Hebrews 13:5).

J is for **Jesus**....*Jesus* came into the world to save sinners...(1 Timothy 1:15).

K is for **kind**. ..be ye [you] *kind* one to another...
(Ephesians 4:32).

L is for **love**....if God so loved us, we ought also to *love* one another (1 John 4:11).

M is for **made**. I will praise Thee [God] for I am fearfully and wonderfully
made...(Psalm 139:14).

N is for **neighbor**....Thou [you] shalt love thy [your] *neighbor* as thyself [yourself]
(Galatians 5:14).

O is for **obey**. Children, *obey* your parents in all things: for this is well pleasing unto
the Lord (Colossians 3:20).

P is for **parents**. Children, obey your *parents* in the Lord: for this is right
(Ephesians 6:1).

Q is for **quiet**....My people shall dwell [live]...in *quiet* resting places
(Isaiah 32:18).

R is for **rainbow**....God said..."I do set My *[rain] bow* in the cloud...
(Genesis 9:12-13).

S is for **sing** a song.....*Sing* praises unto His [God's] name; for it is pleasant
(Psalm 135:3b).

T is for **teaching**....Jesus went about all the cities and villages, *teaching*...
(Matthew 9:35).

U is for **us**....God...loved *us*, and sent His Son [Jesus]...(1 John 4:10).

V is for **voice**....The Lord our God will we serve, and His *voice* will we obey
(Joshua 24:24).

W is for **world**....God sent His only begotten Son into the *world*...(1 John 4:9).

X is for **example**....be thou an *example*...(1 Timothy 4:12).

Y is for **you**. Casting all your care upon Him; for He [God] careth for *you* (1 Peter 5:7).

Z is for **Zacchaeus**....He *[Zacchaeus]*...came down, and received Him [Jesus} joyfully (Luke 19:6).

The stage was set for growing
a true servant of the Lord.

CHAPTER SIX

SALVATION!

At the age of five, already a capable reader, Jonathan had a brief and not entirely happy encounter with the public school system when he entered kindergarten at the Ravensworth Elementary School. His teacher was Mrs. Lea, a grandmotherly lady who clearly loved her work and the children who had been placed in her care. But an indication of problems ahead came when the young student reported to us that the administrator had called an assembly and advised the children that they should not tell their parents about everything that happens in school. This disturbed us. We had taught Jonathan that it was important for us to know all the events in his life since we had a God-given responsibility to nurture, discipline and train our child in the way that he should go. When we heard next that the school wanted Jonathan to be enrolled in the Spanish Immersion Program for Mathematics and Science, beginning in first grade, we decided that despite the strain it would place on our budget it was necessary to have our son in a school environment that matched our values and aspirations. By the start of the next school year Jonathan was enrolled in Fairfax Baptist Temple Academy, on Braddock Road.

The high standards of this private Christian school immediately exposed the fact that Jonathan's quite accomplished reading skills of a year earlier had all but disappeared. In kindergarten, phonics was not taught. For the next several months we struggled together to recapture his lost skills. Sometimes we were reduced to tears of frustration. Then one night it all seemed to come back to him and his reading became fluid again. The next challenge was memory work, since the new school placed an emphasis on the memorization of scripture verses. He took easily to this task: little by little, the powerful Word of God began to germinate in his heart.

On March 7, 1990, the Sunday School lesson was on the subject of salvation and how to serve the Lord. The next day he woke early in the morning and turned on the television to listen to a preacher talk about salvation. The message captured his unwavering attention: God loves everyone but each of us is a sinner separated from God by our sin. To restore this broken fellowship God sent His only Son, Jesus Christ, to live a perfect life in our place and die an awful death on the cross in our place. Yet Jesus did not stay in the grave-after three days He rose again to prove His divinity and the perfection of His sacrifice, which alone is the means to attain eternal life, for those who will receive it. The preacher emphasized that it was Jesus Christ who declared:

I am The Way, The Truth, and The Life,
No man cometh to the Father but by Me.

His heart burning within him, Jonathan carefully repeated the prayer that concluded the sermon: "Lord Jesus, I need you. Please forgive me of my sins. Thanks for paying my debt on the cross. I open the door of my life and receive you as my Savior and Lord. Please take control of my life and make me the kind of person that you want me to be."

The little boy was barely five-years-old, but as he prayed it seemed that the weight of sin lifted from him. He turned the television off and ran excitedly to his father, declaring in a tumble of words that he had asked Jesus Christ into his heart, and it was real to him!

John Leber was alternately delighted and amazed at his son's report and questioned him closely. Did he really understand what he had done? Had he really experienced a life-changing encounter with the risen Jesus Christ? Together, father and son carefully explored the meaning of the words found in John 3:36, "He that believeth on the Son hath everlasting life." Then they joyfully embraced each other.

From that day forward, Jonathan began his spiritual walk in Christ. He was eager to saturate himself with the wisdom and knowledge of God. By the third grade he received the school's Christian character Award, and it seemed he never looked back. Many years later he expressed his thoughts about training children, emphasizing the need to train them in godly ways and immerse them in the Word of God.

"Believers should follow God's methods and examples in the Bible on how to train children," he wrote. "Remember that God knows more than today's experts. Some people say that a parent's good life and sincerity alone will automatically produce godly children, but that is not true. Look at the examples that God gives us to contradict this view-Eli, Noah, Jacob, and David all had problems with their children. Be sure that you are walking in the Lord, because your children are always watching you and they will follow after your example-and be sure that you invest the time and effort to train them."

CHAPTER SEVEN

"He Swam His Way Into Our Hearts…"

Swimming became Jonathan's second passion. A month before his conversion to Christ we joined the Ravensworth Swim and Racquet Club near our home and signed him up for lessons with a swimming instructor. He quickly demonstrated his fearlessness by becoming adept at diving to the bottom of the pool to retrieve pennies and other objects. A year later he was invited to join the club's swim team and quickly mastered different swimming styles, the most memorable of which was the breaststroke because of the chant he learned as he practiced the complex hand and arm coordination: "Pray and scoop the bowl, pray and scoop the bowl!" Soon he was garnering ribbons for his efforts in freestyle, breaststroke and backstroke. As an eight-year-old, he began to compete with children a year older, earning four first place ribbons as a member of the freestyle relay team. He also developed a close relationship with a fellow club member, Katie Van Gilst.

Their unusual friendship was noticed by others. Children at the pool would tease Katie, "You like Jonathan!" But what drew them together was their shared devotion to Jesus Christ-even at that early age they were both looking towards a higher calling of serving their Lord. The close friendship continued through to their high school years, never as boyfriend and girlfriend but as fellow believers supporting each other in their walk with God.

When Jonathan turned twelve he began to teach other children how to swim and his dedication to the sport was evident in the fact that he cheerfully adopted a training regime from 4:30 a.m. to 6:00 a.m. each day. By this time his younger sister, Danielle, was also swimming and coaching others and their parents were hard-pressed to support both their schedules. They dressed for school after their early morning training sessions at the recreation center and ate their breakfast in the car on the way to school.

By the summer of 2003 Jonathan qualified to represent the U.S. Eastern Zones in freestyle competition and the thought began to grow in his mind that he wanted to swim in the Olympic Games. At the end of his freshman year in college he became head coach of his community swim team. We recalled just how much the sport meant to him when we were on vacation together and found him practicing his swimming strokes in his sleep!

He also became an accomplished diver, often competing in higher age brackets as a result of his skill and daring.

But he never overlooked the primary motivation of his life. A swimming friend, Walter Fedrowitz, was introduced to Christ through Jonathan's leadership and example and recalls that Jonathan's goal was to reach everyone he could for the Lord. Others recalled the breadth of his interests and the intensity of his focus on his various pursuits.

One family wrote after his death:

It just seemed that he excelled at anything he did, whether it was swimming, diving, coaching, or his missionary endeavors. And oh, how our children have looked up to him through the years. I do believe that he has taught the breaststroke to most all of the kids in Ravensworth. We remember his horrible bicycle accident and that he refused to stay home because he had kids to teach and a team to coach. What a pillar of strength and courage Jonathan will always be to us, the Imbriglia family."

The mother of a young girl whom he coached wrote a lengthy tribute that speaks volumes, and speaks for many others.

"Dearest Jonathan,
How should I begin? I promised your Dad and Mom that I would write something about you but it has been hard to put it in writing. I

59

would rather talk to you like I did in the summer not too long ago.

News about your plane going down hit me so hard. I could not sit still; I needed to talk to someone. I needed someone to tell me it was not you. Then Alaina sent an email with your voice on the cell phone and I went nuts. How could it be? I remembered calling the Washington Post and the Washington Times and telling them about you; so young, so handsome, so fine and full of life; that you and Alaina were good friends and that you coached Evan and many other little kids at Ravensworth. Until now I still can't believe you are gone. David and I went to the church and saw many old friends there, your parents and sister too. What we remembered most about that night was being able to see the video of you preaching. You were excellent, Jonathan and you were believable and we were so proud of you. You were a grown man, a good preacher and we like what we heard. What a tragic loss!

I missed you so much, Jonathan, this past summer as I went to the gym at Wakefield Rec Center and you were not there to talk to me. You would come up from the pool deck and stand by my treadmill and tell me about your life at college and how much you loved to fly and of course about your improvements in the 50 free. You always had that competitiveness in you. Sometimes we would sit outside in the front of the Center on the bench and we would talk about swimming, about the people who hurt us and how we should forgive them. I enjoyed most when you talked to me about your dream of flying down to the rural areas of Brazil and spreading the Word of God. You really knew what you wanted after you finished college and I was impressed by your determination. What about a girlfriend? I asked. 'She must have the same desire like me and support my dream!!' You answered. A long time ago, I wished that you would ask Alaina out but it is too late now. You were so shy and protective of her and may be it is best that way.

I went to Office Depot and had your graduation photo enlarged to give to your Dad. The lady took one look and asked me if this was the same young man in the news. I started crying and she cried along with me, saying she has two sons and she felt my pain. She refused to take my money and told me how sorry she was for my loss. You see, Jonathan, even a stranger loves you.

When Brittany called and asked for photos of you to make a memorial album, David and I went looking and found about thirty or so pictures. I never saw the final product but I hope it was good and our contribution helped. The photos brought back so many fond memories of you and the time we spent together. I would never forget how upset I was when you fell off *your bike and broke your front teeth; just a few days after your braces were off. Your dad was upset but you were so cool about it. 'It was an accident,' you said.*

Not too long ago, I had a dream and you were walking toward me and started talking to me. In my mind, I said 'You are not here, Jonathan!!' But you were real, the same old Jonathan I knew and we did talk although when I woke up, I couldn't remember what we talked about.

I still go to the gym at Wakefield and look down at the pool for you. Dan, the manager, and I talk about you sometimes. Even the old ladies you used to teach water aerobics talk about you. How could we ever forget you? How could we forget your bright smile and your friendliness toward all people?

So here's to you, Jonathan, my boy! Sweet dreams and I will see you again one day.

With much love,
Thuy McMurray.:

Mrs. McMurray's daughter wrote:

When I look back and think of Jonathan, the first thing that comes to mind is his kindness and friendliness. He has always been someone who has stood out of the crowd. I have known Jonathan ever since I was ten years old, when I joined his summer swim team, Ravensworth.

Jonathan was one of the first people that I met and became friends with. We then grew up together, spending every day in the summer swimming with Ravensworth. We also swam with the same Potomac Valley Swim team, The Potomac Marlins. Also, we carpooled for a while, and it was always fun driving with Jonathan.

Jonathan was a person with a great personality. He was such an easy-going, approachable type of guy. He seemed to be friends with just about everyone. I don't think I have ever met anyone who had anything bad to say about him. From swimming with him, I knew that he was a dedicated and hard worker, who trained eagerly to achieve his goals. He was a great competitor and had an immense amount of sportsmanship. He always had such a positive outlook, and I felt as though I could always go to see him before a race to get ready. On top of that, he was wonderful with children, as all the little kids that he coached simply adored him. He was someone that the team, and especially myself, looked up to and admired.

Time flew by, and before we knew it, Jonathan was off to college. I still saw him occasionally when he was home, either at the pool or the gym. I remember him always talking so passionately about his dreams of becoming a missionary worker. I always admired his selflessness and his desire to spread the Word to others.

I was in school in Australia, when I first hear about what had happened to Jonathan. I was so upset and wondered why something like this had to happen to him. Why did it have to happen to someone who was so young and who had a wonderful and charitable lifetime planned ahead of him? I then realized that life is not fair and that sometimes bad things do happen to good people. Life is a series of tragic losses, but in order to lose something; we had to have had it in the first place, so that the magnitude of each loss then becomes the measure of life's gifts. While Jonathan is gone now, he will not be forgotten. He will always have a special place in my thoughts and heart. I take comfort in the knowledge that he is at last in peace and in a better place.

Alaina.

Another friend wrote simply, "He swam his way into all of our hearts."

The swimmer was also a thinker. Reflecting on his love for swimming in a private journal entry he asked the rhetorical question: "Have you ever needed to go to a place to think or to be alone for a while? A place where you will not be bothered by any distractions? I like to go to the pool. The pool is the one place that I feel at home, whether on vacation or at college. I feel comfortable and safe at the pool and I can think, free of distractions. The pool has a calming effect on me. When you enter the pool area, your nostrils are filled with the scent of chlorine. As you enter the cool, calm water your tightened body begins to relax. While you are swimming, all the worries and stress of your life are put on hold and you can finally calm down. You are also able to talk with God without all the distractions of the world, for a moment you may even feel free from it. After you are done swimming, you hop out of the refreshing water and the weights of the world are dropped back on your shoulders and your quiet, private time is over. Welcome back to the world!"

CHAPTER EIGHT

...AND MUSIC TOO!

It was not enough that Jonathan loved God and loved swimming—he loved music too! He loved to sing. Mrs. Stillwell, his teacher in fourth and fifth grade later remarked, "Great character starts young, and Jonathan was always conscientious about doing his best and being his best whatever he was doing. It was during his two years in my class that his singing ability began to shine."

When he discovered the joy of singing in an organized group he threw himself into it with a passionate intensity. Soon he was winning prizes for his singing. Later, as a teenager, he expressed his thoughts about music in a paper entitled, *The Scriptural Basis for My Musical Choices.*

"I have been taught all throughout my life to love Christian and classical music," he wrote, "but

I really did not have a reason why except that my parents and my pastor said that was the type of music I should listen to. One day in high school at a swim meet a friend of mine asked me, 'Why do you listen to that type of music, instead of alternative rock and stuff like that?' That question haunted me for a while. Then at school some students and the youth pastor were having a discussion on why the youth group does not use Contemporary Christian music (CCM). My youth pastor could not fully answer this student's question. This began my search through the Scriptures for an answer on why CCM and rock music is wrong. I finally found the verse (Romans 12:2) in the Bible that states:

> *And be not conformed to this world: but be ye transformed by the renewing of your mind, that ye may prove what is that good, and acceptable, and perfect, will of God.*

"This verse answered the many questions running through my head. We are to be transformed (changed and different) from the world and the worldly things around us. Christians should be Christ-like, wanting to grow closer to Christ each day and further away from the world. Additionally, in Galatians 5:16-26, we read:

> *This I say then, Walk in the Spirit, and ye shall not fulfill the lust of the flesh.*
> *For the flesh lusteth against the Spirit, and the Spirit against the flesh: and these are contrary the*

one to the other: so that ye cannot do the things that ye would.

But if ye be led of the Spirit, ye are not under the law.

Now the works of the flesh are manifest, which are these: Adultery, fornication, uncleanness, lasciviousness, idolatry, witchcraft, hatred, variance, emulations, wrath, strife, seditions, heresies, envyings, murders, drunkenness, revellings, and such like: of the which I tell you before, as I have also told you in time past, that they which do such things shall not inherit the kingdom of God.

But the fruit of the Spirit is love, joy, peace, long-suffering, gentleness, goodness, faith, meekness, temperance: against such there is no law.

And they that are Christ's have crucified the flesh with the affections and lusts.

If we live in the Spirit, let us also walk in the Spirit.

Let us not be desirous of vain glory, provoking one another, envying one another.

"The idea in this passage is that we should walk in the Spirit and ignore the lusts of our sinful flesh. This will allow us as Christians to serve the Lord much better. Galatians also talks about how we should not have a part in adultery, fornication, uncleanness, lasciviousness, idolatry, etc. These different sins are found and accentuated in the lyrics of rock songs as well as country music. The Bible says that we should not take part in these sins. So, we should not allow our ears to listen to this type of garbage. As Christians, we should strive to inherit and listen to music that adheres to the fruits of the Spirit: love, joy, peace, longsuffering, gentleness, goodness, faith, meekness, and temperance. It should not appeal to our fleshly lust but to our spiritual walk with Christ. The words should be honoring and glorifying to the Lord and not be directed to our selfish desires (the flesh). Ephesians 4:17-24 states:

> *This I say therefore, and testify in the Lord, that ye henceforth walk not as other Gentiles walk, in the vanity of their mind, having the understanding darkened, being alienated from the life of God through the ignorance that is in them, because of the blindness of their heart: Who being past feeling have given themselves over unto lasciviousness, to work all uncleanness with greediness.*
> *But ye have not so learned Christ; if so be that ye have heard him, and have been taught by him, as the truth is in Jesus: That ye put off concerning the former conversation, the old man, which is corrupt according to the deceitful lusts; and be renewed in the spirit of your mind; and that ye put on the new man, which after God is created in righteousness and true holiness.*

"The easiest way for me to explain this passage and how I decide what music to listen to is to imagine myself stuck on a bridge. On the left side of the bridge are all things that are holy; Jesus Christ, and His will for my life. On the right side of the bridge is the world filled with all the worldly pleasures and sins. As a Christian, I know that Jesus Christ set an example for me to live by. I also know that I will never be able to live like Christ, but I can strive to get as close to Jesus Christ as I can (Christ-like character). I just imagine myself on the bridge striving to choose the right music. If the music brings honor and glory to God then the music will bring me closer in my walk with the Lord, but if my choice of music does not bring honor and glory to God I will be hindered in my walk with Him. Every Christian needs to understand this principle and strive to bring their walk closer to Jesus Christ. The one motto that always pops in my head while trying to decide if a certain type of music is Christ-honoring is 'What Would Jesus Do?' If I ask myself this question about each piece of music, it reminds me that I need to understand that I am listening to this music to bring my walk as close as possible to Jesus Christ's walk so that I can have communing fellowship with my Lord and Savior.

"When considering Christian music, there are some key points to review. First Christian music is not meant for the lost but for the believer to express in song his praise, honor and glory to the Lord who provided our salvation. The only method for bringing the lost to Christ is the preaching and teaching of the Holy Scriptures. This is the way God has provided. Contemporary Christian music is watered down, feel good, non-judgmental, worldly, fleshy, cool, and anti-Jesus. It references Christ as he, him, you, and I.

"Contemporary Christian music gives the appearance of political correctness and tolerance.

Believers are warned in the Bible to be discerning and to be aware of people preaching 'another Jesus or another gospel.' These are false teachers.

"Most importantly, this world is not interested in praising the Lord. Secondly, Christian music is for the Lord and is unfriendly to the world. If the music is worldly it is against the Lord. This concept is stated in James 4:4:

> *Ye adulterers and adulteresses, know ye not that the friendship of the world is enmity with God? Whosoever therefore will be a friend of the world is the enemy of God.*

"Christian music gives all the praise, glory, and honor to the Lord, but Contemporary Christian music tends to focus on the musician or singer and how to entertain the audience. The words of Christian music must be clear, the message plain and not enticing believers with fleshly desires, so that it draws the believer away from Christ. The music should draw us closer to the Lord. It should be spiritual food to the soul, admonishing Christians while praising God. It is a serious ministry to the Lord and not entertainment, a talent show, or a performance. As believers, we are to daily crucify the flesh. According to Ephesians 5:19, believers sing unto the Lord, not to the world.

"There are three key ingredients in good music. They are melody, harmony, and rhythm. The emphasis should be on the melody. However, in the case of rock music, rhythm or the beat is the dominant part of music. When this is the primary emphasis it feeds the lusts of our fleshly and physical desires rather than the desires of the Lord. So when it comes to best describing the way we should choose music to listen to as believers, the Bible clearly states in Colossians 3:1-3:

> *If ye then be risen with Christ, seek those things which are above, where Christ sitteth on the right hand of God.*
> *Set your affection on things above, not on things on the earth.*
> *For ye are dead, and your life is hid with Christ in God.*

"We need to seek music that glorifies God-not music that brings glory to this world and the many ungodly things of this world.

"Should Christians view music as amoral? The primary direction of our songs should be to the praise and glory of God as stated above. The question is, can we sing a song to God and bring Him glory? Music is not amoral; there is immoral music, and there is spiritual music."

Elaborating later about the duties of a song leader in a local church, Jonathan added:

"The spiritual objective of a song service is to prepare the hearts of the congregation for the service and to bring glory to God. A song leader's role is to lead the congregation in worship to God. Also, he should prepare ahead of time to make sure that the songs are right with the sermon. The song leader should be excited and smiling while leading the music. Furthermore, he should be organized and know the songs before the songs are played in church. To break up the monotony, a song leader could occasionally use different stunts or "special effects". For example, he could read part of the song or even read a verse that pertains to the song. If the song leader happens to direct a children's choir, the director should love children and have a basic knowledge of music. Also, he should be patient and willing to work with the children by allowing them to sometimes choose a song to sing. First and foremost, the music and words should bring praise, honor, and adoration to the Lord."

CHAPTER NINE

THE TALE OF
THE GREEN MALLET

To add to his musical repertoire, Jonathan learned to play hand bells under the direction of Mrs. Sandy Kester. After his death she interviewed the hand bells and mallets about their experiences with the teenage boy. This is the story told by his first and favorite mallet.

I was born in the Schulmerich factory in Sellersville, PA 1997. I have thousands of brothers and sisters but they are scattered all over the United States and who knows, maybe even around the world. I and one of my brothers were sold to a lovely large church and school in Fairfax, Virginia. We (the mallets) were sent with three octaves of beautiful bells. We were so excited to finally be useful to someone.

We arrived the week before Christmas 1997. When our box was opened for the first time, a whole group of kips were looking in on us all talkative and wide-eyed. We didn't know what to think of them and if the truth be told, they didn't know what to think about us either. We were their first mallets ever. Well, there was a very nice teacher who explained to this group of kids the importance of taking care of us. She said things like: "These mallets are not your property, this is God's property." Also, "We want these mallets to last a very long time and remember that they are expensive to replace."

So after that, I was put back in my home position at G4/A4. There, I was introduced to a nice young man who held that position, Jonathan Leber. He was a sweet-faced, crew-cut, blonde haired guy. My brother and I were very nervous at first with this person. We didn't know if he was going to like us and treat us well.

The teacher set music in front of her students. "Okay, this is it!" I said to my brother. The blonde boy took me up in his right hand and my brother in his left. The group was told to play lightly at the beginning. With the first hit, I said, "Umph", my brother said "Hmph." Not too bad. Just barely a tap. The teacher was counting, "One and two and three and four and…' and the kids were following left, right, left, right. The class period went quickly and we were happily put to bed back in our mallet bag with our other cousins. I thought as I went to bed, "Hey this isn't going to be so bad!"

The next week seemed to come quickly. The boy was smiling as he opened the bag looking for my brother and me to take us back to our position for the class. The teacher announced that this lesson with the mallets would be more difficult. "Oh boy," I thought, "what does that mean?" I soon found out. The teacher was counting "One-e-and-a, two-e-and-a, three-e-and-a, four-e-and-a…" and the kids were following fast left, right, left, right. When the boy started playing quick like that I said "Hey!" and my brother said, "Whoa!" We were in for a wild ride that day. When we were put away for the week at last we lay there in our bag, all achey and bruisey.

"Wow," I thought, "this is going to be hard work with this guy, he really likes to play us with all his might!"

The classes and the weeks passed quickly that year and we got used every single week, sometimes more often. This group of beginner students was so good, they went all the way down to something called "Nationals" in another part of America called South Carolina. What fun it was to see and hear all the other groups down there. I even got to see some of my brothers and sisters and the groups they had been sold to.

As the year had progressed, that sweet-faced boy kept telling the teacher that I was looking ragged and my yarn was looking shaggy. She told him in turn to be careful with me. Well, I could have told her that he was being careful with me, but he was a really diligent and enthusiastic young man. One like she'd never seen before. Others told the teacher to calm him down, that he "got too much into the music," but she never wanted to discourage him. That's what made him special. He put his heart into everything. So time went on to the end of the school year.

One day as the boy was playing me I just couldn't hold on to my hair any longer and my beautiful green yarn fell off, leaving me a white ping-pong-looking Styrofoam ball. The whole class turned and said "Oh!" with a very loud gasp. They stopped and pointed at me and the boy. They had never seen a naked mallet before. I was humiliated to be seen without my beautiful green hair. What was to become of me?

The boy asked the teacher to please let him take me home so he could hang me on his bedroom wall as a "badge of honor."

"No," said the teacher, "*I'm* going to put it up on *my* shelf and whenever any student asks what happened to the mallet, I'm going to tell them about the sweet-faced, crew-cut, blonde-haired boy who played with all his might until the green mallet was no more."

That's not the end of the story. You see, that boy went on to graduate and become a preacher and a pilot. One day he was giving it all he had as usual, doing what he loved, flying a plane to get better and better at it. But things didn't go as he planned. Instead, God chose to take that boy home to heaven.

Though I don't suppose he ever thought of me again after graduation from high school, I stand on top of a bookcase in the hand bell room, surrounded by his pictures, as a monument to his enthusiasm for music and everything else that his hands found to do.

CHAPTER TEN

FIRST SERMONS

Throughout his upper elementary, junior and senior high school years, Jonathan participated in the annual academic and fine arts competitions sponsored by Virginia's Old Dominion Association of Christian Schools (ODACS). His involvement included choir, large group ensemble, small group ensemble, color photography, academic testing, and preaching. This is where Jonathan had his first taste as a preacher.

His first sermon that he preached for competition was entitled:

Not All Ways Lead to Heaven.

Jesus saith unto him, 'I am the way, the truth, and the life: no man cometh unto the Father, but by me.'
—John 14:6

The world tells us that there are many ways or roads to God. You must pick a way and you'll reach God. However, according to the Bible, not all roads lead to God. This verse tells us that there is only one way, one path, and that is through Christ.

Enter ye in at the strait gate: for wide is the gate, and broad is the way, that leadeth to destruction, and many there be which go in thereat: Because strait is the gate, and narrow is the way, which leadeth unto life, and few there be that find it.
—Matthew 7:13-14

1. **JESUS IS THE WAY**
    a. Man's Way:

There is a way that seemeth right unto a man; but the end thereof are the ways of death.
—Proverbs 16:25

Think of all the possible paths we have-the road of immorality, the avenue of alcohol or drug abuse, the way of ungodly friends. But in Christ, there is an alternate path…the right road starts with Via Dolo- rosa-the way of the cross. It starts with salvation.

    b. God's Way:

Thou hast made known to me the ways of life; thou shalt make me full of joy with thy countenance.
—Acts 2:28

The Lord shall establish thee a holy people unto Himself, as He hath sworn unto thee, if thou shalt keep the commandments of the Lord thy God, and walk in His ways.

—Deuteronomy 28:9

God's way is straight and narrow and is directed by God's Word.

II. JESUS IS THE TRUTH

Jesus is the Living Word according to John 1:1:

In the beginning was the Word and the Word was with God and the Word was God.

Not only is Jesus the Word but His words that He spoke were Truth.

Psalm 145:18 declares:

The Lord is nigh unto all them that call upon Him, to all that call upon Him in truth.

And the Word was made flesh, and dwelt among us, (and we beheld His glory, the glory as of the only begotten of the Father,) full of grace and truth.

—John 1:14

For the law was given by Moses, but grace and truth came by Jesus Christ.

—John 1:17

Sanctify them through thy truth: Thy word is truth.

—John 17:17

Not only is Jesus the way and the truth, but He is also the Life. He is the Bread of Life, the Resurrection and the Life, the Giver of Life, the Creator.

III. JESUS IS THE LIFE

And this is the record, that God hath given to us eternal life, and this life is in his Son.
He that hath the Son hath life; and he that hath not the Son of God hath not life.
These things have I written unto you that believe on the name of the Son of God; that ye may know that ye have eternal life, and that ye may believe on the name of the Son of God.
—1 John 5:11-13

The Philippian jailer asked a question that brought a fitting answer.

Sirs, what must I do to be saved?
And they said, Believe on the Lord Jesus Christ, and thou shalt be saved, and thy house.
And they spake unto him the word of the Lord, and to all that were in his house.'
—Acts 16:30-32

So then faith cometh by hearing, and hearing by the Word of God.
—Romans 10:17

Jehoshaphat stood and said, Hear me, O Judah, and ye inhabitants of Jerusalem; Believe in the Lord your

God, so shall ye be established; believe his prophets,
so shall ye prosper.'
—2 Chronicles 20:20

We must believe and obey the teachings of God's Word based on the fact that it is Truth. Examine your life. You may think that being religious is the answer. No! You won't go to heaven unless you accept God's gift of eternal life. Here are the ABC's of Salvation:

A. ADMIT you are a sinner:

For all have sinned and come short of the glory
of God.
—Romans 3:23

Ask Jesus Christ to forgive your sins. There is a penalty to be paid for sin. Either you will pay it, or you must accept Christ' shed blood on the Cross as payment for the penalty of sin. The choice is yours.

For the wages of sin is death; but the gift of God is
eternal life through Jesus Christ our Lord.
—Romans 6:23

Sanctification of life does not earn eternal life; it is still God's gracious gift.

B. BELIEVE in Christ who died for you:

For God so loved the world, that He gave His only begotten Son, that whosoever believeth in Him should not perish, but have everlasting life.
For God sent not His Son into the world to condemn the world; but that the world through Him might be saved.'

—John 3:16-17

C. CONFESS Him as Savior and Lord:

If thou shalt confess with thy mouth the Lord Jesus, and shalt believe in thine heart that God hath raised him from the dead, thou shalt be saved.

—Romans 10:9

He who confesses that Jesus is Lord affirms His deity.

For with the heart man believeth unto righteousness; and with the mouth confession is made unto salvation.'

—Romans 10:10

These are simultaneous actions: one inward (the heart) and the other outward (the mouth).

If we confess our sins, He is faithful and just to forgive us our sins and to cleanse us from all unrighteousness.'

—1 John 1:9

A characteristic of that first sermon was its heavy emphasis on Scripture. The next year, when Jonathan was asked again to preach an evangelistic message for the ODACS competition he continued this emphasis. He believed the most exemplary life is nothing without Christ, and the revelation of Christ shone from the pages of his Bible. His second ODACS sermon was entitled:

BEHOLD THE LAMB OF GOD.

The next day John seeth Jesus coming unto him, and saith, Behold the Lamb of God, which taketh away the sin of the world.
And looking upon Jesus as he walked, he saith, Behold the Lamb of God.

—John 1:29 and 30

I.   We must ask ourselves, what did John the Baptist mean by this saying-"Behold the Lamb of God"? I believe he understood that God and God alone provides the remedy for the sinful state of man. Just as Abraham knew God would provide in answer to his son's fateful question in Genesis 22:7-8:

And Isaac spake unto Abraham his father, and said, My father: and he said, Here am I, my son.
And he said, Behold the fire, and the wood; but where is the lamb for a burnt offering?

And Abraham said, My son, God will provide him-self a lamb for a burnt offering; so they went both of them together.

Only God could restore the fellowship lost in the garden of Eden when Adam and Eve sinned, by providing the sinless lamb of God, Jesus Christ, who was tempted in all areas in which man is tempted (the lust of the flesh, the lust of the eyes, and the pride of life). Hebrews 4:15 declares:

For we have not an high priest which cannot be touched with the feeling of our infirmities; but was in all points tempted like as we are, yet without sin.

II. John understood the sinfulness of man. He was in the wilderness baptizing people for repentance for the remission of sin. Luke 3:3-4:

And he came into all the country about Jordan, preaching the baptism of repentance for the re-mission of sins; As it is written in the book of the words of Esaias the prophet, saying, The voice of one crying in the wilderness, prepare ye the way of the Lord, make his paths straight.

III. John understood that no man was without sin. He would agree with the statements made by Paul, James, and John in their writ-ings, that man falls short of God's standard. 1 Peter 1:16:

It is written, Be ye holy; for I am holy.

One sin, no matter how great or small, makes a man a sinner and brings him under a death sentence both physically and spiritually. James 2:10:

For whosoever shall keep the whole law, and yet offend in one point, he is guilty of all.

For all have sinned, and come short of the glory of God.
—Romans 3:23

If we say that we have no sin, we deceive ourselves, and the truth is not in us.
—1 John 1:8

As a result of sin, we die physically-but there is good news. Romans 6:23 promises:

For the wages of sin is death; but the gift of God is eternal life through Jesus Christ our Lord.
—1 John 1:8

If you accept God' gift, you will obtain eternal life.

IV. John understood that the Lamb of God paid the price for our salvation. Isaiah 53:5-6 reads:

But He was wounded for our transgressions, He was bruised for our iniquities: the chastisement of

our peace was upon Him, and with His stripes we are healed.
All we like sheep have gone astray; we have turned every one to his own way; and the LORD hath laid on him the iniquity of us all.

Not only did Christ pay our penalty for sin willingly but it cost Him pain.

And almost all things were by the law purged with blood; and without shedding of blood is no remission.

—Hebrews 9:22

Without the shedding of the blood of Christ, there is no salvation. Christ, the sinless Lamb of God paid the price required of God to redeem man from his depraved state and restored the fellowship with God that was lost in the garden of Eden when man sinned.

V. John understood the importance of repentance in order to have a right relationship to God. This requires man to confess his sin.

That if thou shalt confess with thy mouth the Lord Jesus, and shalt believe in thine heart that God hath raised him from the dead, thou shalt be saved.
For with the heart man believeth unto righteousness, and with the mouth confession is made unto salvation.

—Romans 10:9-10

Right relationships deal with true repentance.

If we say that we have no sin, we deceive ourselves,
and the truth is not in us.
If we confess our sins, He is faithful and just to
forgive us our sins, and to cleanse us from all
unrighteousness.

—1 John 1:8-9

God created us and loved us so much that He
provided a way to restore this right relationship.

But God commendeth His love toward us, in that,
while we were yet sinners, Christ died for us.

—Romans 5:8

For if by one man's offence death reigned by one;
much more they which receive abundance of grace
and of the gift of righteousness shall reign in life
by one, Jesus Christ.

—Romans 5:17

Salvation is free with no strings attached. It is
only by faith like a child that we believe that Jesus
died for our sin. He is the only way. John 14:6:

Jesus said, I am the Way, the Truth, and the Life, no
man cometh to the Father but by Me.

Jesus was sinless and He bore our penalty of sin
on the cross.

For I delivered unto you first of all that which I
also received, how that Christ died for our sins

according to the Scriptures; and that He was buried,
and that He rose again the third day according to
the Scriptures.

—I Corinthians 15:3-4

Each person will stand before God someday and be judged. If you have accepted Christ as Savior and Lord, God will see the righteousness of Jesus in you, but if you have not received Christ into your heart, you will pay the punishment for your sin, which is the eternal wrath of God. Hebrews 9:27-28:

And as it is appointed unto men once to die, but
after this the judgment; so Christ was once offered
to bear the sins of many; and unto them that look
for Him shall He appear the second time without
sin unto salvation.

—I Corinthians 15:3-4

VI. John understood that Jesus Christ, the Lamb of God is the great "I AM."

Worthy is the Lamb that was slain to receive power,
and riches, and wisdom, and strength, and honour,
and glory, and blessing.
And every creature which is in heaven, and on the
earth, and under the earth, and such as are in the
sea, and all that are in them, heard I saying, Bless-
ing, and honour, and glory, and power, be unto Him
that sitteth upon the throne, and unto the Lamb for
ever and ever.

—Revelation 5:12-13

The believer will be eternally thanking God for salvation and praising and worshipping the Lamb of God, Jesus Christ. In Revelation 7: 9-10:

> *After this I beheld and, lo, a great multitude, which no man could number, of all nations, and kindreds, and people, and tongues, stood before the throne, and before the Lamb, clothed with white robes, and palms in their hands; and cried with a loud voice, saying, Salvation to our God which sitteth upon the throne, and unto the Lamb.*

Not only will the saved be praising the Lamb of God but they will be singing! Revelation 15:3:

> *And they sing the song of Moses, the servant of God, and the song of the Lamb, saying, Great and marvelous are thy works, Lord God Almighty; just and true are thy ways, thou King of saints.*

The saved will willingly be praising the Lord and bowing down to the Lamb of God but the unsaved will be saying something quite different! Revelation 6:16:

> *And said to the mountains and rocks, Fall on us, and hide us from the face of Him that sitteth on the throne, and from the wrath of the Lamb.*

Not only will the unsaved ask to hide but they will war against the Lamb as written in Revelation 17:14:

*These shall make war with the Lamb, and the Lamb
shall overcome them; for He is Lord of lords, and
King of kings; and they that are with Him are called,
and chosen, and faithful.*

Obviously, God, the Creator, will win in the end.
We see a glimpse of what heaven is like, described
in Revelation 21: 14-22:3:

*And the wall of the city had twelve foundations,
and in them the names of the twelve apostles of
the Lamb.*

*And he that talked with me had a golden reed to
measure the city, and the gates thereof, and the
wall thereof.*

*And the city lieth foursquare, and the length is as
large as the breadth; and he measured the city with
the reed, twelve thousand furlongs.*

*The length and the breadth and the height of it are
equal.*

*And he measured the wall thereof, an hundred and
forty and four cubits, according to the measure of
a man, that is, of the angel.*

*And the building of the wall of it was of jasper: and
the city was pure gold, like unto clear glass.*

*And the foundations of the wall of the city were
garnished with all manner of precious stones.*

*The first foundation was jasper; the second, sap-
phire; the third, a chalcedony; the fourth, an em-
erald; the fifth, sardonyx; the sixth, sardius; the
seventh, chrysolyte; the eighth, beryl; the ninth,
topaz; the tenth, a chrysoprasus; the eleventh, a
jacinth; the twelfth, an amethyst.*

And the twelve gates were twelve pearls; every several gate was of one pearl: and the street of the city was pure gold, as it were transparent glass.

And I saw no temple therein: for the Lord God Almighty and the Lamb are the temple of it.

And the city had no need of the sun, neither of the moon, to shine in it: for the glory of God did lighten it, and the kings of the earth do bring their glory and honour into it.

And the gates of it shall not be shut at all by day: for there shall be no night there.

And they shall bring the glory and honour of the nations into it.

And there shall in no wise enter into it any thing that defileth, neither whatsoever worketh abomination, or maketh a lie, but they which are written in the Lamb's book of life.

And he shewed me a pure river of water of life, clear as crystal, proceeding out of the throne of God and of the Lamb.

In the midst of the street of it, and on either side of the river, was there the tree of life, which bare twelve manner of fruits, and yielded her fruit every month: and the leaves of the tree were for the healing of the nations.

And there shall be no more curse: but the throne of God and of the Lamb shall be in it; and His servants shall serve Him.

This service will be for all eternity. However, there is only one way to know that you will be in this wonderful place. The gift is free. You must be saved. Just follow the simple A, B, C rule-you must *admit* you are a sinner, *believe* Christ died for you, and *confess* your sins to Christ.

Are you willing to follow the simple A, B, C rule? As Joshua would say 'Choose you this day whom you would serve'. As for me, I choose to believe on the Lord Jesus Christ, the perfect Lamb of God which taketh away the sin of the world. What about you? Do you want to know Jesus Christ as your personal Savior? You can, if you will confess with your mouth that you are a sinner and believe that Jesus Christ paid the price for your sin with the shedding of His own blood on the cross of Calvary. Then, ask Christ to forgive your sins and to come into your life as Lord and Savior, believing He will save you. He will because He saved a poor sinner like me.

CHAPTER ELEVEN

FIRST FRIENDS

From the time Jonathan started attending Fairfax Baptist Temple Academy, he and Jason LeGrand became pals. Although Jason's family later moved to Missouri, Jonathan treasured having him as a friend in his elementary school years. Then the LeGrand family moved back to northern Virginia and the friendship was renewed.

"On the first day, Jon showed me around and re-acquainted me with our old classmates," Jason recalled. "That year we shared many experiences, including singing the national anthem in the Rotunda of the Senate offices!"

But what impressed Jason the most was Jonathan's story that his father was one of the original team members of the football team from the movie, *Remember the Titans*.

"He could see I didn't believe him so he proved it to me by inviting me to see the movie and telling me all about the history of it. I understood it was very important to him that he knew I trusted his word."

During their senior year the two boys worked closely together on the student council. "I don't know if we improved the school very much, but I know that both of us learned a lot about leadership and had a lot of fun in our lunch meetings with Mr. Hansen, the principal. Jon was always outgoing and never afraid to try something new, as he showed with some of the outfits that he wore on spirit days. At our senior banquet, I will never forget the white and black wingtip shoes that he wore with his outfit!"

As graduation drew near the friends talked about their plans for the future. They both shared a desire to join the air force, but the call of God led them in a different direction. Jonathan went off to Maranatha Baptist Bible College in Wisconsin to study missions and aviation, and Jason went to Bob Jones University in South Carolina to study pre-medicine.

"We would catch up with each other over Christmas breaks and the summers, mostly to see if either of us was dating yet! Then the day came when I got the news that Jon's plane had gone down overnight. At first, I remember being concerned but not too worried because I knew that Jon had made it down alive and that he was an incredible swimmer. But when I heard that the lake was near freezing that night, I began to pray very hard that God would spare Jon's life. We know now that God had other plans for him."

Jason remembers that his friend always had a passion for the ministry.

"It was not a superficial, flashy passion, but rather it was something you sensed from him, a deep commitment. In the sermon that he preached on the New Years' Eve before his death, Jonathan spoke about how real our God should be to us to stir us to action for Him.

"That sermon has taken on new meaning and life for me because Jon gave that invitation with his own life. In His sovereignty, God is mightily using his life to call others to go to the mission field in his stead."

Another classmate from upper elementary school through graduation went on to the same Bible College with Jonathan. Amanda Darby remembered their excitement at the thought of soon graduating from Maranatha together.

"I remember him preaching about his God, the Solid Rock, in high school. And it was certainly evident throughout college that Christ was his Rock. He wanted to go on telling others about Christ. Jon's life portrayed his dependency on the Rock, even in his final moments."

Jonathan also became firm friends with Matthew Hawes. Matt was slightly older but that was not a barrier to a relationship that he described as a true friendship "beyond price."

"Many people spend a lot of their lives looking for the kind of friendship we enjoyed," Matt later told Jonathan's parents. "He was a true and loyal friend. I knew Jonathan for many years, and there were many experiences that we shared together. Both of us loved to compete in the area of sports. The two of us were on the soccer team at Fairfax Baptist Temple Academy for many years, and had a lot of good times both in practices and in games. We were on the championship team in 1999. And we sang in choirs together—once it came down to just him and me holding down the bass section! Jonathan also spent some time with me as I prepared to preach for the final time in ODACS Regional Competition and we were both part of a mission's trip to Alaska in 1997. In 1998 we visited Pensacola Christian College in Florida.

"It almost goes without saying that one of Jonathan's greatest interests was swimming. I was always amazed at how he could keep up the pace that he did, and his efforts were later greatly rewarded. He not only became good, he became one of the best at what he did, and he taught others how to try to do the same. He took what he learned and he put that back into others' lives. There are many who for years to come will line up at swim meets and use the techniques that he showed them as they strive to succeed in their own races.

"I only saw him sporadically after I graduated from high school the year before his graduation, but I vividly remember the very real change that took place in Jonathan's life when he went on his mission's trip to New Zealand. He returned having made the decision to go into missionary aviation and he never looked back. He poured himself into his goal, and, like the other things that he set his mind to, he became well skilled in piloting airplanes.

"The last time that I ever saw Jonathan was at a pick-up basketball game. My last memory of him was seeing him surrounded by a group of girls!

"Months later, I could not believe the news when I checked my answering machine and heard of his death. Not him. No way. As the days went by and the truth began to sink in, I was tossed by different emotions. One in particular was the regret that I felt for not spending the time that I should have spent with him after I graduated. There was a feeling that something like this was not supposed to happen to someone our age. Focusing on my work during those last few weeks of my undergraduate career became something extremely difficult to do.

"Then one day as I was reading through the Gospel of Luke for a college assignment I found the comfort I had been looking for when I came to Luke 20:37-38. In this passage Jesus is debating the resurrection with the Sadducees. He tells them that God *is not a God of the dead, but of the living: for all live unto Him.*

"The point that Christ makes here is that the God Who *was* the God of Abraham, Isaac, and Jacob is *still* the God of Abraham, Isaac, and Jacob. Those who have died have done nothing more than pass from this holding-tank into the true reality. Jonathan's passing hit me hard, but, when I read these verses, it came flooding into my soul that Jonathan was just as alive as I was, and actually much, much more alive than I'll ever be on this earth. He wanted to serve God with his life, and now he was serving at the very feet of God Himself. The God that *was* Jonathan's God is *still* Jonathan's God. Right now, Jonathan is part of that crowd of witnesses who cheer the rest of us on.

"This changed my whole perspective on the events that had occurred. Were they still tragic? Yes. Were they still very painful? Yes. But a Christian does not sorrow as those who have no hope. The eternal side of the whole event finally came into view.

"Now when I look back at Jonathan, I think of a person that loved life and that lived it to its fullest. He pretty much always had a smile on his face, and he tried to make the people around him happy as well. The response to his passing was amazing, and it is awesome to think of all those people that were inspired by Jonathan to take the Gospel to the nations. For every soul saved under their ministries, Jonathan will receive more rewards for having had a part in those conversions. The work that he wanted to do on this earth is still very much going to get done, and on an even grander scale than he probably ever imagined.

"Thanks, Jonathan, for your friendship and for all of the fun times we had together. Thanks as well for the inspiration that you provided then and still provide now. I miss you greatly, but I look forward to the ages that we will have to catch up with each other in eternity. See you soon."

Another of Jonathan's classmates through his entire school career was Anthony Mandela. His first reaction to the news of Jonathan's death was shock, then something approaching despair.

"The realization didn't fully sink in until I saw the story on the news and heard Jon's voice over the cell phone. I broke down in front of the screen and did something I hadn't done in a long time: I cried. So many emotions and mental pictures flooded my mind and heart, as I thought about Jonathan and the friendship we had shared over our lifetime. I have never had anything so close and so real hit home like this did. I became frustrated and even angry as I struggled with how to deal with what I had just seen on the TV.

"Jonathan and I shared a close relationship, especially the last 4 years of his life. I remember touring the streets of Chicago with him and looking out from the Sears tower as we shared our ambitions and struggles with each other. We both had so much to look forward to and such bright futures to anticipate as we anxiously sought to know how God would uniquely use each of us in accordance with His will and master plan.

"Jonathan and I have worked together the past two summers and have 'hung out' many times since graduation. I have shared his testimony here at my school with many people. He was a great and loyal friend to me. We have grown, struggled, failed, and succeeded many times through the course of our friendship and I thank God for the time he had on this earth and the encouragement and testimony he has been to so many people who have had the privilege to come into contact with him. Even as I work through the pain, I can see how God is using this situation to teach me so much in my life right now."

At his graduation Jonathan was one of several "honor graduate" speakers (his GPA was 3.70). His words again had a prophetic ring to them as he thanked God for the free gift of His salvation.

"This is the most important gift for man to accept and the most important decision anyone can make...To the graduating class of 2002, we are now single adults and we must be responsible in the use of our abilities and the choices and decisions we make. Always keep your focus on the Lord. Romans 12:1-2 says,

> *I beseech you therefore, brethren, by the mercies of God that ye present your bodies a living sacrifice, holy, acceptable unto God, which is your reasonable service.*
> *And be not conformed to this world, but be ye transformed by the renewing of your mind, that ye may prove what is that good, and acceptable, and perfect will of God.*

"Satan will send problems your way but take them to the Lord. Jesus is my Rock, as stated in my life verse, Psalm 18:2. The words to the song "I Know Who Holds Tomorrow" by Ira Stanphill clearly tell us to place everything in God's hands:

'I don't know about tomorrow, I just live from day to day.
I don't borrow from its sunshine, for its skies may turn to gray.
I don't worry o'er the future, for I know what Jesus said, and today I'll walk beside Him, for He knows what is ahead.
Many things about tomorrow, I don't seem to understand: but I know who holds tomorrow, and I know who holds my hand.'

"So fix your eyes on the Lord and He will see you through. Then give the glory to God for what He has done and realize that your unknown future is in safe hands of the all-knowing God. The song I just quoted and this little poem summarizes everything I just said:

'I know not what the day may bring, tomorrow waits unknown.
But this I know, the changeless Christ, my Lord is on the throne.'

CHAPTER TWELVE

PLANNING FOR THE MISSION FIELD

As Jonathan struggled with conflicting priori-ties in his life he wrote to several missionaries, asking them for insights about missions work. Dr. Royce Vick responded with careful answers to each of the young man's many questions.

Most missionaries receive their training after they get to the field, Dr Vick explained, suggesting that Jonathan should work on the staff of a church as a youth pastor and involve himself with what-ever mission program the church supports. Most importantly, he advised, "Be involved in the local soul winning ministry of your church. If you are not a soul winner at home, you will not be a soul winner on the field."

Dr. Vick said he considered service on a foreign field to be the highest calling of God, since it meant taking the Gospel to a land and people who have never heard, and building local New Testament churches where there are none. But he stressed the importance of first attending Bible College.

"You should take all courses offered. Most colleges offer a one year course in missions. I recommend that every summer, you should visit a mission field and a missionary for two or three weeks."

He warned, however, that missions work was difficult.

"The number one problem is cultural shock. You are thousands of miles from home, you don't understand the language, you don't understand the customs and culture, the food is different, the smell is different, the houses are different, and there are diseases that you have never heard of. But don't let this discourage you. I have been on the field for 31 years, and I guarantee you, God is able. Learn how to PRAY, and get in contact with God before you go."

Explaining why he had given his life to the work, despite the difficulties, Dr. Royce said he did not choose to be a missionary. "God chose me. If there was anyone who was not qualified, it was me. I flunked at least two years of school. I dropped out of high school in the 11th grade, and joined the Navy. I was not saved until I was 26. I was the worst sinner that has ever been born. Christ saved me in March 1970, and God called me to preach in April that year during a mission's conference. Then He burdened my heart for a foreign field. I surrendered my life, and my family, and all that I owned, and waited for His leadership. I visited a veteran missionary in Mexico, and the Holy Spirit said to me, this is the place. I returned to Texas, finished my schooling, did a short deputation, and was in the field, full time, the last of March 1971, barely a year after my salvation."

The highest personal qualification required of a missionary was "a passionate concern for lost souls, especially for those who do not have the opportunity to hear the Gospel, like we do here in the States. Don't worry about your ability. If God has called you to be a missionary, He will equip you. God will not lead you where He cannot take care of you."

Based on the advice he received from Dr. Royce and other missionaries, Jonathan set down his own thoughts on the subject.

What it Takes to be a Missionary

In today's society, there is no great emphasis in the church for missionaries. Currently, the missionaries in the field are becoming elderly and are coming off the mission field not able to return. Therefore, the need is even greater for new missionaries to go to replace the aging missionaries as well as to go to new places around the world.[1]

The matter is not that God is not calling young men and women. He is, but the fact is that few are responding positively to His call to obey and go.

---

[1] John Leber, Rebel Gospel Ministries, interview by Jonathan Leber, took notes, Springfield, Va., 21 December, 2001.

Today, Christian parents discourage their children from making a full-time commit to become a missionary and encourage them to seek other vocations instead. However, each believer needs to be actively engaged in taking the gospel of Christ to a lost and dying world. The goal of the church must be to prepare young men and women for the possibility of full-time service through educating them in the mechanics of missions, should God call them into the field.[2]

Not everyone is called to the special calling but all must be prepared to go if called upon. Once a young person has been called by God to be a missionary, he must act by receiving the proper training. Then get prepared to go and serve on the mission field.

"Missionary" comes from the Latin word, *mitto*, which means "to send." So the definition of the word *missionary* is "one who is sent on a mission; especially, a person sent to do religious work in some territory or foreign country."[4]

Of course, before a person can become a missionary, the individual must be saved. Once saved, he must have received the call from God to be a missionary, just like the Apostle Paul was called by God. He must be willing to yield to God's will by preparing to go to wherever the Lord leads.

[2] Ibid.

[3] J. Herbert Kane, The Christian World Mission: Today and Tomorrow. Grand Rapids, Michigan: Baker Book House Company, 1981, 139.

[4] American Heritage Dictionary, 840.

After the young person acknowledges God's call to be a missionary and responds positively, his next step is to receive proper training. He must be grounded in the Word of God. Remember, Jesus taught and discipled His apostles during His ministry on earth knowing that they would be His witnesses to the lost when He was finished doing the Father's will. He knew precisely when they were ready to go into the world to spread the Gospel.

Secondly, the individual must get prepared to study the people, their language, their culture and other barriers that may arise while on the mission field. A good way to learn more about the people and their country is to take a mission trip. This experience will allow the individual to see the pros and cons of a country and its people. Another important purpose of a mission trip is that it will burden the person of the need for more missionaries around the world.

The training for a missionary begins at Bible College. There the missionary will learn more about the God's Word, church planting, counseling, leadership, and team building. Pastor Scott Silsbee, missionary to New Zealand, believes that every missionary or pastor should have at least a bachelor's degree in the area of ministry or Bible. He also recommends that a potential missionary should go on to get a master's degree.[5]

---

[5] Pastor Scott Silsbee, Questionnaire

Another good way for a missionary to train for the mission field is for him to become a pastoral intern. Here the missionary-in-training learns directly from the pastor the valuable lessons to prepare him for the time when he actually goes to the field. On the other hand, the most useful form of training for a missionary is actual field experience.

Probably the most important decision, after responding to God's call and preparing for the mission field, is to know where God wants the missionary to serve. The decision should be made after much praying and seeking of God's perfect will to be done in his life. A good way to help a missionary determine if he has made the right choice on a mission field is to have him visit that mission field. Then, the individual and his family can know whether they can adapt to living in that country as well as know the culture barriers they may encounter. However, one's focus should be on telling people about Jesus Christ and maturing the believers, no matter what the culture is, because God's Word never changes.[6]

Once one has finished his training and knows the mission field where God wants him to serve, he is ready to choose the right mission board. Finding the right mission board should be like finding the right Bible college to go to.[7] First, must pray to God for the wisdom in choosing a mission board. Then, seek a mission board that has the same beliefs and

[6] Smallman, William H. "Communicating with Awareness," Harvest, Winter 1999, 11.
[7] Silsbee, Questionnaire.

standards. Lastly, find a mission board that has the same Biblical doctrines and beliefs.[8] The potential missionary needs to be associated with a mission board that he likes and knows will support him. Once he has selected a mission board, applied and been accepted, he must begin deputation. Deputation is very important because it is by visiting various churches that a missionary will be financially supported. When he goes on deputation, he should only visit those churches that hold to the same Bible doctrines and standards. Also, he should know which churches he thinks may support him while he is on the mission field and concentrate on visiting them first. Once sufficient support has been raised, the missionary is ready to go.

The last step is to go and serve on the mission field where God has called him. The missionary's ultimate goals must be to start a church, train a native to be the pastor, and then move on to start another church. That means the missionary must have a strategy. He should be willing to befriend the natives, so that they will trust him. During the same time period, he should be passing out gospel literature and going on door to door visitation. Visitation is a vital part of soul-winning. He could possibly invite people in for a meal or just to talk. The key is to gain their trust and friendship. Eventually, the missionary will be ready to have Bible studies and/or group meetings either in his home or in a designated meeting place. As the church grows,

---

[8] Ibid

he must be actively training his replacement to take over the church so that he can move on and start more churches.

A prime example of a missionary who was successful in spreading the Gospel was the Apostle Paul. First, he was called of God. He accepted that challenge and preached the gospel wherever he went. He served God by serving men. While he was on his missionary journeys, he maintained close contact with his home churches that prayed and/or supported him. He knew that as a missionary he could not cover the whole earth. Therefore, he concentrated on starting churches in cities where large crowds could be found. If people were not responsive to the preaching of the gospel, he moved on. Once a church was established, he moved to another town to begin the task again. However, Paul took fellow workers to assist in establishing churches. He definitely believed in teamwork. Before he died, Paul trained Timothy to continue the missionary work.[9]

So Paul's success started with the call of God to be a missionary. Then he had to be completely dedicated to doing the will of God. Finally, he had to rely solely on the power of the Holy Spirit. The power of the Holy Ghost gave him the ability to present the gospel to all men.[10]

---

[9] Kane, J. Herbert. Christian Missions in Biblical Perspective. Grand Rapids, Michigan.: Baker Book Co., 1974, 73-83.

[10] Ibid, 85-89.

In summary, then, a missionary must first be called of God, receive proper training and preparation in order to go to the mission field. Next, he must obey and go. Once on the mission field, he must preach, teach, and disciple. Without the proper mission board and the prayers and financial support of the home churches, the lost will not hear the good news of salvation.

Remember that our Lord came to seek and to save the lost and now is the time to serve the Lord. Work for the Lord while it is day for soon the night will come when it will be too late to work.

CHAPTER THIRTEEN

MISSION'S WORK

In 1997 the whole Leber family joined Maranatha Baptist Church on a mission's trip to Alaska. It was Jonathan's first real taste of life on the mission field and although he clearly enjoyed the experience it did not seem to make a deep impression on him. Despite making a commitment to full-time Christian service at the age of 14, he became distracted with what the world had to offer and by his junior year in high school he decided to apply for entrance to the Air Force Academy and the Naval Academy. We were deeply concerned. Life in the military was not in our plans for him and we were convinced that neither was it God's design. But instead of lecturing Jonathan we jumped at what we saw as a God-given opportunity to influence him in the right direction.

The McLain family, missionaries to New Zealand, visited Fairfax Baptist Temple in the spring of 2001 and something about them and their story of life on that far-away mission field captured Jonathan's interest. Missionary Bob McLain suggested that we should contact his coworkers, the Silsbee family, who were currently in New Zealand working in the Hamilton church planting ministry. Coincidentally, Mrs. Lori Silsbee had taught Jonathan music in the upper elementary grades at Fairfax Baptist Temple Academy before she and her husband and their daughter Heidi joined the work in New Zealand. Now they were willing to take Jonathan under their wing and let him see first hand what it would be like to work as a missionary. He was 16-years-old when he set off on his great adventure.

The intention was for him to be fully involved with the work, singing, teaching and preaching, while partially supporting himself by babysitting and doing menial chores. Some of the activities planned for him included teen and young adult visitation, helping in the preparation of the McLain's home for their arrival back from furlough and passing out tracts inviting young people from the local high school to attend church.

A week after his arrival in New Zealand he preached his first sermon, at a meeting for high school students.

JESUS CHRIST, THE ALTERNATIVE ROCK

The LORD is my rock, and my fortress, and my deliverer; my God, my strength, in whom I will trust; my buckler, and the horn of my salvation, and my high tower.

—Psalm 18:2

You are probably asking yourselves why I chose this theme. Well, it is because no matter what the world offers you, you will still feel empty. Alternative means substitute, our other options, our choice between two things. Let me tell you why I believe that Jesus Christ is our alternative to everything this world has to offer—He is an Alternative Rock on which we can build truly useful lives.

First, the world offers power, but power will leave you heartless. In Exodus we read that Pharaoh's heart was so hardened toward God and God's chosen people that he allowed Egypt to be plagued. If we look at Pharaoh's stubbornness in refusing to free the Israelites, we see a great example of how power can make a person heartless. There were ten plagues that God pronounced each time Pharaoh refused to let God's people go, but it took the death of his son to finally weaken Pharaoh's hard heart. Yet even then he changed his mind. Pharaoh still did not want the Israelites to be free. His power left him heartless. So he and his army chased after the Israelites and the entire Egyptian army ended up dead at the bottom of the Red Sea.

Next, the world offers lust, but lust will leave you loveless. The best example of this is found in 2 Samuel 11:2-25. The story tells of King David's lust for Bathsheba that led him to commit adultery. She became pregnant as a result and David summoned Uriah, Bathsheba's husband, to come home. But instead of sleeping in his own house, he sleeps at the door of the king's house. David then gets him drunk but still he does not go to his home. Finally, David writes a letter to have Uriah put on the frontlines of the hottest battle to have him killed. Worse yet, David has Uriah deliver the letter to the Captain of the army. When David hears that Uriah has been killed, he marries Bathsheba. But the Lord is displeased. God sends Nathan, a prophet, to King David to rebuke him by using a parable that is outlined in 2 Samuel 12:1-14.

David repents of his sin, but is still scarred for life. We must remember that our sins can be forgiven but we will suffer the consequences of sin. In contrast to David's lack of love we see the definition of true love in the love of Christ, who willingly shed His blood and died for us when we did not love Him.

Thirdly, money will leave you comfortless. I Timothy 6:10 warns:

> For the love of money is the root of all evil: which while some coveted after, they have erred from the faith, and pierced themselves through with many sorrows.

If I were to give you twenty dollars, you would probably be happy right then. Later, if you spent that twenty dollars on something you really wanted, it would probably keep you happy for a while-at least until you get bored with your new toy. What happens once you get bored? You become unhappy! So you want more money and more things. This is why we cannot rely on money or things to make us happy. Money ultimately leaves us comfortless. Instead, we should rely on our relationship with Jesus Christ and be content and satisfied with what we already have. Praise the Lord and be thankful. An attitude of gratitude is much better and it encourages us to be positive by counting the blessing that we have, one by one. When we do, we will be surprised by what God has done.

Fourth, drugs will leave you senseless. God instructs us in Ephesians 5:18:

And be not drunk with wine, wherein is excess; but be filled with the Spirit.'

We read further in 1 Corinthians 6:19-20:

What? Know ye not that your body is the temple of the Holy Ghost which is in you, which ye have of God, and ye are not your own?
For ye are bought with a price: therefore glorify God in your body, and in your spirit, which are God's.

Remember that once you are a believer in Christ, your body is not yours but is now indwelt by the

Holy Spirit. Thus it is prudent that you be careful what you do with your body and what you put into your body because you should be doing it to glorify the Lord who saved you. This concept is emphasized in 1 Corinthians 10:31:

> *Whether therefore ye eat, or drink, or whatsoever ye do, do all to the glory of God.*

So, young people, think before you do, and ask yourself if what you intend to do will be honoring and glorifying to the Lord.

Lastly, Jesus won't leave you, regardless! In Hebrews 13:5 we learn:

> *Let your conversation be without covetousness; and be content with such things as ye have: for He hath said, I will never leave thee, nor forsake thee.*

God promises that He will be there for you regardless of your problems, temptations, trials, circumstances, or situations. Just call upon Him and He will answer you. According to Proverbs 18:24:

> *A man that hath friends must show himself friendly; and there is a friend that sticketh closer than a brother.*

That friend is Jesus. The song writer wrote declared joyfully in that old familiar hymn, 'What A Friend We Have in Jesus.' He truly is there and He will see us through. No matter what the world and flesh send your way, as long as you trust in God, He will take care of you. When things go wrong in our lives, we need to take them to the Lord in prayer and ask for His help and strength. With God all things are possible. Matthew 19:26 declares that some things may be impossible to men, 'but with God all things are possible.' This same thought is expressed in Mark 9:23 when Jesus promises that all things are possible to him that believeth. The key is that you must believe, with a child-like faith. Remember that you and God make a majority! Jesus Christ is our Alternative Rock! The Lord is our rock.

Shortly after preaching this message Jonathan had a heart-to-heart talk with the Silsbee's about what he planned to do with his life. They shared their personal testimonies about how they had felt God leading them into the ministry, the choices they made and the joy that came from serving the Lord. They discussed Jonathan's desire to swim, to fly, and to be in the ministry, and the resulting conflict of purpose. They reminded him that God doesn't want us to be miserable and that we will truly be happy when we surrender to Him and do His will for our lives.

Later Jonathan recorded that it was during this conversation when he began to realize that God could take his two greatest passions—to fly and to be a minister of the gospel—and use them both for His purposes. A few days later he shared a message with a teen group that reflected his new-found understanding of the possibilities that lay ahead.

Staying Ahead
II Corinthians 4:1-8.

Staying focused in the ministry can become difficult at times. To keep on doing what God has called you to do, continuing on for the Lord despite the trials, can't be accomplished by will power. You can't just determine to do it and succeed. Even though it is nice to have people encouraging you to live for God, they can't keep you doing it! You have to 'know how.'

I don't suppose there is anyone more qualified to teach us how to focus on our service for the Lord than the Apostle Paul. Here is a man who endured some of the greatest hardships possible for Christ. He was hated by both Jews and Gentiles. He was misunderstood and attacked even by other Christians. Eventually he was executed for nothing more than preaching Jesus Christ. Yet, at the eve of his life, he was able to say, "I have fought a good fight, I have finished the course, I have kept the faith."

Problems occur in everyone's life. How do Christians stay focused in their service to God? We can learn a lot from Paul's example.

I.   PAUL ACCEPTED THE MINISTRY GOD GAVE HIM. (II Corinthians 4:1)

A.   Paul was not in an easy ministry.
He was not accepted by the other Apostles for several years. He was constantly challenged

and questioned even by the other Apostles throughout his ministry. He suffered shipwrecks, beatings, stoning and jailing, on a regular basis. But he accepted the ministry God gave him.

B. The context of this verse is in view of the trials he faced because of his ministry.

In Chapter 3, Paul answers the question as to whether or not he needed to have a letter of commendation from the other Apostles. Paul's ministry was being attacked by some within the Corinthians church. Yet, despite all that, he simply writes, seeing we have this ministry...we faint not.

C. We would do well to learn from this to accept whatever ministry we have.

Sometimes all of us get to looking around and wishing we had it like someone else. We wish we could be the pastor. We wish we could be the teen leader. We wish we could sing as well as some who have talents in music. If we want to continue for the Lord, the first step has to be that we accept the position that God gives us in His work! We need to come to the place where we accept whatever ministry God chooses to give us. Verse 1 hints how to do that: "...as we have received mercy of the Lord, we faint not." The truth is, whatever position we have in the plan of God, for the church and for His ministry, is a merciful position! We could be the ones who are outside. We could be the ones facing hell, no the ones trying to keep souls from going there! So Paul accepted the ministry that God gave him.

II. PAUL HAD A PROPER VIEW OF HIS PROBLEMS. (II Corinthians 4:8-9)

These were the verses that got my attention as I prepared this message. Paul draws four contrasts here:

A. Troubled–not distressed. The word "troubled" means to be crowded or pressured. The word "distressed" means to be in calamity. In other words, he is saying that he is squeezed, but not squished! There is tremendous heat generated on the exterior of the Concorde airplane when it flies at supersonic speeds. The temperature on the outer surface of the plane can get to 127 degrees C (261 degrees F) even though the outside air temperature is -56 degrees C (-169 degrees F). The expansion caused by this heat makes the plane 9 inches longer at cruise speed than at rest. The cabin floor of the aircraft is built on rollers and doesn't expand, and four air conditioning systems keep the inside comfortable. While the outside of the plane is undergoing tremendous stress, the inside climate remains constant.

Paul described our 'outward man' as perishing under the heat of great pressure, while our 'inward man' is renewed day by day.

B. Perplexed–not in Despair. The word "perplexed" means at a loss. The word "despair" means completely lost.

C. Persecuted–not forsaken. The word "persecuted" means to oppress or harass. The word "forsaken" means deserted or abandoned.

D. Cast down–not destroyed.

Paul is saying, "Sure I've got problems, but I am not defeated!" I have fallen a few times, but I have always been able to get back up! I have had some times when I wasn't sure which way to turn for a while, but I have never been so lost that I couldn't eventually get out of it! Paul never allowed his trials to completely overwhelm him. Likewise, we too must come to the place where we recognize that the trials we face are not totally devastating! They may hurt. We may not enjoy them. We might have wished we did not have to go through them, but there isn't one of them that has to destroy us!

For the Christian, even the ultimate trial of losing our life isn't really a defeat, but a victory! Now, we face trials from many different angles, like physical trials when our bodies suffer, or social trials or when we suffer at work or with our relationships outside of church. We even face spiritual trials, but we can still keep our faith. We need to keep these trials in perspective and remember they could be worse!

Paul comforted the Hebrews and challenged them to go on for the Lord despite their problems by saying to them, "Ye have not resisted unto blood, striving against sin." (Hebrews 12:4).

Paul kept on going for God and finished his course because he kept his problems in perspective and didn't allow them to overwhelm him.

III. PAUL HAD HIS FOCUS ON THE RIGHT THINGS.

In II Corinthians 4:10-18, there are three things I want to point out to you, but in reverse order.

A. Look at the Eternal, not the Temporal.
   2 Corinthians 4:18 reads:

While we look not at the things which are seen,
but at the things which are not seen,
for the things which are seen are temporal;
but the things which are not seen are eternal.

So many of our troubles could be resolved if we had our eyes on heaven, not on earth. I understand how difficult that is. I struggle with it every single moment of my life. Paul said in Romans that the sufferings of this present time are not worthy to be compared to the glory that shall be revealed in us. All he was saying was that we ought to look for the heavenly and eternal things, not the earthly and temporal things! Jesus said we should not lay up for ourselves treasures on earth, where moth and rust corrupt, and thieves break through and steal, but to lay up treasure in heaven, where neither moth nor rust corrupt, and where thieves do not break through and steal. What He was saying was that we ought to be striving to do things that will last for eternity not for the here and now. Much of the reason we struggle with the Christian life, and one of the reasons some people give up on their course in life, is that they get their eyes fixed on how things are today, right now. If that is how Paul looked at things:

- He wouldn't have been willing to give up his career in the Pharisee's religion for Christ.
- And he wouldn't have been willing to give up his associate pastor's position in Antioch to be a missionary church planter.
- And he wouldn't have been willing to give up his freedom to be a blessing to the poor saints in Jerusalem.
- And he wouldn't have been willing to give up his life to keep his testimony for Jesus Christ!

Paul could endure because his eyes were fixed on heavenly and eternal things, not on earthly and temporal things! He was content to suffer some losses here in order to have more rewards waiting in heaven!

B. Look at others, not self:
   2 Corinthians 4:12 reads

So then death worketh in us, but life in you.

Paul was willing to go through the trials that he did, and hang in there for the Lord because he was concerned more for others than he was for himself. Paul said he became all things to all men that he might by all means save some. Paul's concern in life was not for himself and how he fared physically, but for others and how they fared spiritually! He was willing to suffer any trial, any hardship, and any difficulty so long as he was still seeing souls being saved and lives rescued from hell and torment in order to receive eternal life with Jesus Christ!

C. Look at Christ's Living, not dying:
2 Corinthians 4:11 reads:
For we which live are always delivered unto death for Jesus' sake, that the life also of Jesus might be made manifest in our mortal flesh.

One of the differences you'll find between us and the Catholics is that they use a cross with Christ still hanging there. We use a cross with Christ who has come off it! While we do not want to minimize what Christ did when He died on the cross, we also don't want to get stuck there. Christ not only died on the cross, he was buried in a tomb, and He rose again, He rose triumphantly, He rose victoriously! His triumph translates to our triumph. Today His victory translates to our victory. Today, His glory works for our glory, too!

If all we picture, when we picture Christ, is Him hanging on the cross, we will have a dead and defeated religion. However if, whenever we see Christ, we see Him as Stephen did, in heaven, standing at the right hand of the Father, we will see Him as He is-a Living God! Faith and hope in our living Lord is the number one tool to keep us focused. Just as Paul accepted the ministry God gave him, we need to accept the ministry that God has given us.

Secondly, just as Paul had a proper view of his problems, we also need to have a proper view of our problems.

Thirdly, just as Paul focused on the right things, we to need to focus on the right things.

Problems occur we understand that, but if we maintain the proper focus God will help us and bless our ministries.

Stay Focused!

When Jonathan returned to the United States from his mission trip to New Zealand, he was changed. He had experienced the spiritual coldness and blindness of people in an far-away land and was burdened by the great need to "go into all the world." Sometime during that brief visit, he fully yielded his life to the Lord. Other dreams and ambitions would be laid aside.

CHAPTER FOURTEEN

COLLEGE LIFE

In late August 2002 the budding young missionary arrived at Maranatha Baptist Bible College
in Watertown, Wisconsin, firmly set on the most
important formative experience of his life. He
quickly made friends—and a few enemies. His personality had a marked eccentric tilt. People either
liked him or disliked him, but it was impossible to
ignore him. He would affably insert himself into
any conversation or group and while he had the
respectfully polite demeanor typical of a teenager
raised in a strict Christian home, his collection of
strident scripture verse ties and outrageous mail-
order belt buckles spoke unmistakably of a strong
independent streak.

Often, he would reveal only one side of his
multi-faceted identity to those acquainted with him:

Preacher-boy; pilot; student; wrestler (in his junior year he joined the wrestling team); swimmer; coach; taskmaster; prankster; dutiful Christian; friend.

He sat always at the back of his class and his thoughts were clearly sometimes elsewhere—perhaps literally in the clouds—yet his assignments were completed on time and his papers and essays were crafted with a fluid ease that exasperated some classmates whose work-load was considerably less than his double major in Bible and Aviation. The latter course required him to enroll in the nearby Wisconsin Aviation School. In addition to his heavy program of studies he found a job as assistant swim coach for the Watertown High School. He was pursuing all of his passions at once without any apparent stress. On the contrary, his ready smile and mischievous nature meant that he always had time for a prank. He was, observed a close friend, completely at ease with himself.

His first milestone at Bible College was a name change. Jonathan became "Ace" after Dale Mundt, a fellow freshman who would soon become one of his closest friends, introduced himself to others in the dorm and discovered that four were named John or Jonathan.

"That night, while a couple guys from across the hall were sitting in our room, I told Jonathan that he needed to find a new name. There were just too many Johns! I told him I wasn't going to call him Jonathan or Jon anymore. So if he wanted me to address him, he would have to find a new name.

Everybody started laughing, and we sat around trying to figure out a nickname for him. He told us that he wanted to be a pilot. After a while, we settled on 'Ace.' I don't think that anyone expected it to stick, but whenever I introduced him to people, I introduced him as Ace. Eventually, he just gave up trying to explain. Everybody knew him as Ace. By the time his accident was announced on campus three years later and his name was given as Jonathan Leber, most people didn't realize that it was him!"

The prospect of becoming a pilot was exhilarating to "Ace", but he was equally excited by the opportunity to impact the lives of his swimming students—and in that world he was known as "Jon".

The head coach of the swimming team, former Navy SEAL instructor Mark J. Kruse, described his new assistant as "one of the best people" he had ever met.

"When Jon first walked into the office of our Athletic Director for his interview, his maturity belied his 17 years. He carried himself with command but not arrogance. He answered questions with knowledge and intelligence. He knew his chain of command and how he fit into it without having been in the military. He was friendly and polite and couldn't have been more perfect for the job than if he'd been 25 or 30. This was a product of superior upbringing, regardless of his spiritual affiliation. One of the questions I asked him was if he could plan a 14-week workout schedule for brand new swimmers. Keep in mind he was only 17-years-old, younger than some of my swimmers. His answer was yes. Not maybe, or if you help me. He said yes! That is a mark of confidence."

Jonathan had of course been coaching since he was 12-years-old, often working with others not much younger than himself. His practical experience helped him to get the necessary cooperation from all the swimmers Mark Kruse assigned to him.

"There was never any doubt who was in charge. Sometimes we would go to meets and the other coaches would ask me who my injured swimmer was, not realizing that he was a coach. They were always surprised that I could let him work independently with his group of swimmers without having to supervise him more closely."

In his third year as a coach the Watertown High School team took the Conference Championship Meet and showed every sign of being a dominant force in the conference for years to come.

In a tribute to Jonathan after his death, Mark Kruse described him as a "different" kind of Christian.

"He took people at face value for their actions and contributions, not their affiliations. Jon never held himself aloof, never attempted to make anyone feel a lesser being due to a religious preference or lack of it. I never saw Jon make anyone feel self-conscious or uncomfortable. Quite to the contrary, Jon went out of his way to make everyone he met feel comfortable around him. I doubt that anything could have gotten in the way of Jon and his God, but by the same token, he wasn't going to be the one to force the issue with anyone. Everyone knew how Jon felt about his religion, but he never expected anyone to feel the same as he did. His feelings were very personal to him and he allowed others to discover their own feelings without forcing them into a corner."

Yet Jonathan enjoyed soul-winning. Since he was majoring in Bible with the aim of becoming a pastor/missionary, he would go street witnessing with other students as part of his Personal Evangelism course. His relaxed approach to strangers he met encouraged them to engage with him in conversation and to listen as he presented an outline of the gospel.

His professors at College found him equally engaging. His English teacher, Traci Mayes, was struck by his willingness talk to her outside the classroom.

"He often made a point of chatting with me at church. English is not usually a student's favorite class and many students prefer to avoid my presence when they can. Jon was friendly and polite every time he spoke with me, whether at church or at school. This was true throughout the years he was here as a student. And he nearly always had a smile or friendly expression on his face. To me, that pleasantness demonstrates the love of the Lord in a person's heart."

Professor Dr. Dwayne Morris was struck by Jonathan's clear focus on his goal of becoming a missionary aviator.

"I first had Jon in Biblical Interpretation class. Every now and then I saw him weary-eyed in class and asked what was wrong. That was how I came to learn of his heavy study schedule, including his flying lessons, and his desire to serve in missions. It was so exciting to hear, and I remember coming home and informing my wife of this young student who had real spiritual goals and was doing something about them.

"Since his death I have often challenged young men to take Jonathan's place. He was a good and godly young man. I'm looking forward to seeing him again."

Dr. Bruce Meyer, who taught Doctrine and Homiletics, was struck by the love his friends had for him.

"He shared his enthusiasm for life; his love for God, ministry, and people; and his interest in spiritual growth. After the accident many of his friends went over to Milwaukee to walk the beach in search of his remains, which was their tangible way of demonstrating their love for him one more time."

Professor David Saxon said Jonathan came to his office only once.

"He was struggling somewhat with his grade in my Theology II class (he was passing but not doing as well as he wished), and he told me that he planned to take a flight to New York. He was going to miss class on Friday, and he wondered if doing so would damage his chances in the class. His attitude was respectful, and I believe that he would have canceled the trip had I insisted he be in class. However, I did not think missing one lecture would hurt him, and I have always thought college students gain educational benefits from a variety of experiences. So I approved his going on the trip and reassured him that there was still time to improve his grade as finals loomed on the horizon."

It was the last time he would see his likeable young student.

For Emily Zielke, a fellow student, Jonathan redefined the word "outgoing".

"He was a joy to be with in class. I had several classes with him, and I was always amazed at his knowledge of whatever topic we happened to be studying. He usually added his own opinion under his breath as well (which was always worth a much needed laugh). It just came naturally to him. He acted as though he never studied, yet he knew the information."

She was struck by his original outlook on life.

"He wasn't satisfied to follow the status quo. Instead, he needed to figure things out for himself. I don't think that Jonathan claimed one specific 'social group' whom he mixed with exclusively at school. He was friendly with everyone."

But some disliked him. For one thing, he made studying seem effortless. Particularly galling to several classmates was the ease and speed with which he produced essays and papers.

"The guy could write a Bible paper in a matter of two hours," Emily laughed. "When most of us would turn in our papers Jonathan had not even picked his topic. He would go to the computer lab and polish off a paper in no time, when the same work took many of us more than a week to do. The first time this happened, before I knew him well, I was sure that he would get a bad grade, but to my surprise, he managed a solid A. That always frustrated me, but Jonathan knew the Bible and he knew how to explain it.

"He was confident and comfortable about who he was. He made his own fashion, and he didn't worry about 'fitting in'. If only more of us could figure that out. I don't ever remember him having a bad day. He always smiled, and he always stopped to chat with just about anybody—even if he was late for class. Jonathan served a Big God, and it was evidenced in his life!"

His facility in producing papers also impressed his close friend Dale Mundt.

"There were times when he would have a two page paper and a four page paper that he hadn't even started writing, and I would have a three page essay due. He would start at 9:00 or 9:30 in the evening and would finish all of his work by 11:00, maybe 11:30. I would still be working on my 3 pages when he got up in the morning to go work out. I have never been able to write like that! I always make tons of mistakes the first few drafts, and I'm never happy with what I wrote. Ace would just start typing, and an hour later, four flawless pages would come out of the printer."

Shamar Bailey saw a different side of him.

"Ace was a very talented swimmer with a lot of goals, and I am a wrestler with a lot of goals. Because we each competed in an 'individual' sport, we could identify with each other and the need to be self-driven, especially in the off-season. Because of this, we trained together a lot. We would run distance and sprints. We pushed my car at times for a change in the type of workout we were doing, in order to develop our lungs, shoulders, and legs. Aside from that, we always lifted weights together and would bounce different kinds of workouts off of each other. Many times, these workouts would be very tiresome when doing them on our own, but with each other they were enjoyable."

Jonathan's circle of friends extended to various workers on campus, including Mrs. Lynn Barnett, who worked in the dining hall.

"He used to come into the kitchen to get his lunch. My friend Jill and I would talk to him for a few minutes before he had to leave. I enjoyed the visits so much, especially when we would talk about life with the Lord. Jonathan meant so much to me."

Surprisingly for one so young and carrying such a heavy schedule, he maintained close friendships even beyond campus. Satish Chacko was at college in Chicago yet Jonathan would occasionally check on him to see how things were going.

"I had made many promises to keep in contact with friends that I had known from high school, but once college started those good intentions fell by the wayside," Satish remembered. "I lost touch with a lot of people. The one exception was Jonathan. When he heard that I was going to be in the Midwest, he was very excited because he went to school in that area of the country as well. The fact that hundreds of miles separated us did not impress him much! Every couple of months, he would call me to catch up and see how things were going and we became even closer friends, despite the distance between us. It was exciting to hear how life was going at Maranatha, and whenever I talked with him I was always amazed with all the things that he was able to do, including swimming, flying, staying on top of academics, and still having time to enjoy himself.

"Jonathan spent the night in my dorm on three different occasions, and those were without a doubt some of our best times together. He could converse with and relate to anyone! Whenever Jon would come over, I would introduce him to a wide variety of people and he showed genuine interest in anyone that he talked to. That had a profound affect on the people that he interacted with. He knew how to fit into any situation. On the other hand, he wasn't willing to compromise on what he knew to be right. People were impressed with the way that he held himself and respected him for what he believed in."

His unique concern for others was expressed in a special way for his close friend Dale Mundt, who joined the military after his freshman year of college and was shipped to Iraq at the end of 2003. Jonathan had previously played matchmaker between Dale and Jessica Van Hall and the two were married on December 17, 2005.

"Dale was interested in two girls," Jessica remembered. "I was one of them. Dale trusted Ace's advice implicitly so naturally he turned to him for help in choosing between the two. Even though he did not know me very well then, Ace saw something in me and told Dale he would be making a mistake to choose anyone else!

"Ace and I were never that close until Dale left for Iraq. When I say that we were not close, I mean that we had only a surface relationship. When Dale got shipped overseas I think we both replaced him for each other. Ace needed to be around someone who loved Dale as much as he did, and I needed someone who knew Dale in a way that I had not yet been able to explore—a person who knew some of his past and completely trusted him. Ace saw how alone and afraid I was and decided he would watch out for me. He especially did not like it when other guys flirted with me. Whenever he thought a guy was 'too friendly' he would just walk up to him and stand there with his arms crossed. So many times he came out of absolutely nowhere just when I needed him!

"There is always a point in time where your friendship takes that first step to something deeper and more meaningful. That step happened late one night—or I guess I should say early one morning—when my phone rang and woke me up out of a sound sleep. Still not quite awake, I heard Ace on the other end and I knew instantly that something was wrong. He asked if Dale was there. 'No, Dale is in Iraq; you know that,' I told him. 'I know,' he replied. 'I was just hoping that for some reason he would answer.' My heart broke just hearing how despondent and miserable he sounded. I asked him what was wrong, and he went on to tell me how a girl that he had been seeing had broken his heart and abandoned him for some other guy. I knew how crazy he was about her and since I had once been in a painful breakup, I shared in his hurt. We stayed on the phone for hours till early in the morning discussing how much breaking up stinks.

"The last couple months that Dale was in Iraq were extremely difficult for me. Ace knew that nights were the hardest time for me and that it was easy to get caught up in self-pity and cry myself to sleep. Every night at 10 o'clock he would call me to make sure I was okay, and we would talk about memories of Dale.

"It's amazing to look back now and see how Ace was always there for me. So many times, Bible college students get caught up in their personal accomplishments and wear their spirituality on their sleeve, so to speak. Ace was so different to kids who lose the big picture of life and get caught up in themselves. He spent so much of his time giving to others and investing in people. He would say that he never spent more that two hours on a paper because he believed that while school was important, there was more to life than writing papers! It sounds like such a cliché to say that he spent every moment to the fullest, but it is true. He never wasted time. His love for God was evident in his priorities and in his spirit but he would never arrogantly flaunt his spirituality.

"The last time I saw him I was walking out of chapel, and just like his style, he came up out of nowhere and slugged me on the shoulder. As he walked past smiling, he winked at me and said, 'Have a good weekend. I'll see you later.'

"Ace was about to make his last flight. That first week after the accident I called his cell phone every day and left voice messages hoping that somewhere, he could hear me. My one comfort is that I *will* see him later."

CHAPTER FIFTEEN

LIVING PURE IN AN IMPURE WORLD

Jonathan was a healthy, active and attractive young man. He had girl friends and girls who were friends. Like his contemporaries, he struggled against temptation and the constant pressure of a society that placed a low value on celibacy and moral purity. But unlike those who were his contemporaries in age, not in heritage, he was strengthened in the battle by a solid grounding in God's Word and the leadership and example of his extended Christian family—parents, pastors, teachers and fellow church members. Though he might fall, he knew how to pick himself up again and where to go for encouragement and counsel.

He believed Christian education provided an important moral foundation and protection against societal pressure, especially in the early, formative years of a child's life.

"Christian education is a safe place," he argued, "although Scripture does not say that Christian education is the only way-as a matter of fact the Bible does not even mention Christian schools. But it does say that it is the parents' responsibility to train up their children in the ways of God. The roots of this instruction are evident in early American education-our schools were never intended to be godless. Harvard, Princeton, and Yale were all founded to train pastors, missionaries and godly school teachers who would faithfully preach and teach the gospel—but look at what has become of these universities today. They now teach humanism, which has a highly negative affect on young people. Our future leaders are disrespectful to authority, self-centered, lacking in discipline and fixed on a worldly perspective rather than a Biblical worldview."

Jonathan's Biblical worldview included a perspective on dating that would cause the average American teenager to choke in disbelief.

"If God plans your future as a single person, He will guide you and use you. On the other hand, if God wants you to get married, He will send you a mate when the perfect time comes. That's where courtship comes in—and it's a lot different than dating.

In short, dating does not involve parents. It is a new movement that started in the early 1900's. Courtship requires parental involvement. Parents arrange the couples. Parents approve of the dating couple. The aim is marriage, not just having fun.

"Marriage is on the minds of almost every college student. It is the next step on the paths of our lives, when a young person leaves the security blanket of parents and cleaves to the love of a spouse. The important aspect of marriage that we tend to forget is that as we spend more time together, we begin to learn about and care more about each other. This mirrors our relationship with God."

At the time of his death he was working on a sermon that explored the subject of moral and sexual purity, based on Psalm 119:9-11:

> How can a young man cleanse his way?
> By taking heed according to Thy word.
> With my whole heart have I sought thee:
> O let me not wander from Thy commandments.
> Thy word have I hid in mine heart, that I might not
> sin against Thee.'

I have heard people ask on many occasions, "Why don't we see power in our churches anymore?" I believe it is because we are impure in our hearts. God cannot use a polluted vessel. Look at James 3:11-12:

> Does a spring send forth fresh water and bitter
> from the same opening?
> Can a fig tree, my brethren, bear olives,
> or a grapevine bear figs?
> Thus no spring yields both salt water and fresh.

This passage is referring to the tongue, but the principle is the same. A polluted spring cannot produce fresh water. God has called us to purity and holiness. Without purity, we cannot experience God's power. Romans 12:1-2 tells us to present our bodies as a living sacrifice holy and acceptable to God. Do not be conformed to this world but be transformed by the renewing of your minds. This is how we align ourselves and find the perfect will of God. If we do not take care to renew ourselves, we will soon be conformed to this world and become polluted in our hearts and minds. Jesus said in Matthew 24: 37-39 and 42-46:

> *But as the days of Noah were, so shall also the coming of the Son of man be.*
> *For as in the days that were before the flood they were eating and drinking, marrying and giving in marriage, until the day that Noah entered into the ark, and knew not until the flood came, and took them all away; so shall also the coming of the Son of man be…Watch therefore: for ye know not what hour your Lord doth come.*
> *But know this, that if the good man of the house had known in what watch the thief would come, he would have watched and would not have suffered his house to be broken up.*
> *Therefore be ye also ready; for in such an hour as ye think not the Son of man cometh.*
> *Who then is a faithful and wise servant, whom his lord hath made ruler over his household, to give them meat in due season?*
> *Blessed is that servant, whom his lord when he cometh shall find so doing.*

Jesus' reference to Noah comes from Genesis 6:5-6 which reads:

And God saw that the wickedness of man was great in the earth, and that every imagination of the thoughts of his heart was only evil continually. And it repented the Lord that He had made man on the earth, and it grieved Him at His heart.

Jesus warned that in the end times, the world would become as it was in Noah's day when God had to intervene. The entire world was morally bankrupt. All we have to do is take a look around us and we can see Jesus' prophecy unfolding. There are many ways that we can have sin in our lives, but none leads to spiritual decay faster than immorality. Today, we live in a society that is completely obsessed with sexual immorality. You cannot walk past the magazine rack in a grocery store without being bombarded with sexual images. What used to be hidden inside the covers is now displayed boldly on the cover. You can't avoid exposure to sexual advertising. All around us are TV shows, commercials, movies, magazines and an innumerable list of abuses of sexuality that pervert sex from God's intended design and make living a godly life difficult.

So how can we keep our ways pure in an immoral world? There is absolutely no way to avoid becoming polluted by the non-stop bombardment of sexuality, without a consistent time of cleansing by renewing your mind in God's Word. We live in a time similar to that described in Genesis 6:5:

The Lord saw that the wickedness of man was great
in the earth, and that every intent of the thoughts
of his heart was only evil continually.

It is not easy to have a pure heart in this world, but we do have the promise, "Greater is He that is in you, than he that is in the world" found in 1 John 4:4. What we really have to decide is what we value most. In James 4:4 we are warned that friendship with the world is to be at war with God. 1 John 2:17 adds that the world is passing away, and the lust of it; but he who does the will of God abides forever.

If the world is passing away, it clearly is not wise to choose the world over God! It is also important to realize that sinful pleasures will not satisfy. They may briefly gratify, but they don't satisfy. There is always an empty void left behind. This is because God has designed us to have fellowship with Him. Only God can satisfy. If pleasures are where our affection lies, then when the pleasures are gone, so is what we have valued most. We are then left empty.

The next lie we are told is that if we go a little farther, we will be content. The reality is that we are being drawn into the infinite trap of Satan's hall of mirrors. Satisfaction through sin is a mirage and always appears to be one step out of our grasp. Only God can fulfill the promise of Psalm 36:7-8:

How excellent is Thy lovingkindness, O God!
Therefore the children of men put their trust
under the shadow of Thy wings.

152

They shall be abundantly satisfied with the fatness of thy house; and thou shalt make them drink of the river of thy pleasures.

Pleasure was designed by God and can only be truly fulfilled by God. It is only found in the path of life and the path of life is only in God's presence (Psalm 16:11). If you cannot remain in God's presence, then you will never find the path of life that God has designed uniquely for you. If you can't be pure in heart, you can't abide in God's presence because Jesus promised that the pure in heart would be blessed for they shall see God (Matthew 5:8).

I personally struggle with things that pollute my mind and seek to destroy my spiritual life. The vast majority of Christians struggle in today's immoral society. With very few exceptions, each of us echoes the same feelings of discouragement, guilt, and hopelessness. We want to live pure lives, but the trap has been set and some are enslaved by these desires. Most Christians do not want to have lust as a part of their lifestyle nor do they want impure hearts. Churches and Christians need to take notice: This problem is not going away and it will only get worse with the direction society is heading. It is the church's responsibility to pave the way to deliverance through Jesus Christ. Only at the foot of the cross can these burdens be removed.

Most people would be completely shocked if they knew just how widespread this problem is within the church. But Jesus said that He came to preach deliverance to the captives and promised that the truth would make us free.

How do we become free when we feel enslaved? Freedom is only found in Christ. It doesn't matter what compulsive behavior we have, Jesus has the power to make us free in Him, through a personal relationship with Him. Without that relationship, everything else is limited because we are limited by our own strength. Then once we are free from our passions, we must put our faith into practice. There are four key areas that we must commit to if we expect to overcome sin and live pure lives, free in Christ.

1. Commit to study the Scripture:

How can a young man cleanse his way?
By taking heed according to Thy word.
With my whole heart have I sought thee:
O let me not wander from Thy commandments.
Thy word have I hid in mine heart,
that I might not sin against Thee.
—Psalm 119:9-11

We cannot renew our minds without God's word. God equates His word with Himself. If we don't have any interest in God's word, the same will be true with our interest in God. God won't reach out to someone who resists Him. He will call us to come, but will not take hold of us until we choose to draw near to Him. Scripture memorization is a key part of study. The psalmist said that he hid God's word in his heart. If you commit to consistently memorizing Scripture, it will change your life. You would be amazed at how much you will memorize if you review memory verses once on the way to work and once on the way home. Read the Bible daily. The Psalms and Proverbs are good starting points for someone who is not accustomed to studying the Bible.

But when it comes to study and memorization, there are a few pitfalls to be aware of. Most people who commit to these study disciplines see a tremendous spiritual growth, but once the emotions fade they begin to postpone study times and soon abandon all their study habits completely. Like everything else in our spiritual lives, feelings should not be our guide. Discipline is when we commit to follow through even when we don't feel like it. Don't overwhelm yourself, but commit to a timeframe that you can handle and build from there. Once you get to the point where you consistently study even when you don't feel motivated, you will begin to experience sustained growth in your spiritual life.

2. Focus on Jesus Christ:

Where our focus lies is where we are going. Resistance is futile if we are looking at temptation. Repentance is the key. Repentance is merely changing direction by turning towards God. You don't always have to be in sin to repent. Repentance is not groveling in self-loathing. Repentance is not striking a bargain with God. It is not putting off sin until a later date or clearing up guilt with the intent to go back. Repentance is committing to a change of focus. It is taking my eyes off what pleases my flesh and changing my focus away from selfish motives and committing to God's plan by putting Jesus at the center of my world. If I am focusing on the world, the world will be my god. I will always give in when I am distracted unless I turn away from the temptation. The problem most of us have is that we are willing to turn our eyes away but we leave our mind on temptation. Resistance is futile when we are in this frame of mind. What we are really doing is trying to find a smaller compromise that allows us to give in a little without feeling like we are giving in. Sometimes we don't want to give in, but we don't think to refocus on Christ. Then resistance is like pushing a heavy weight off our chest. We may be strong at first, but in a short time, we begin to tire and soon we loose the battle.

Resistance based on Scripture is not to push temptation away, but to turn from temptation and toward Jesus Christ. At the point we turn toward God, we are not pushing away from temptation but pulling toward God. The Bible promises that if you draw near to God, He will draw near to you. This is clearly expressed in James 4:8-7:

Submit yourselves therefore to God.
Resist the devil, and he will flee from you.
Draw nigh to God, and He will draw nigh to you.
Cleanse your hands ye sinners,
and purify your hearts, ye double minded.

According to this passage, the key to resistance is to submit to God, then resist. It is the turning to God that enables us to resist because it is only by His power that we are able to resist. We must change directions and change our focus. When we draw near to God, He will cleanse us and give us the ability to live pure lives and get off that double-minded roller coaster ride. In James 1, we are told that we are tempted when we are drawn away by our own lusts and enticed. We are first drawn by our eyes. You cannot focus on Jesus and be drawn away at the same time. You can only focus on one thing at a time. The only thing that stands in your way is your will. Until you are willing to let go of selfish desires, you can never trust God to fulfill your desires by the abundance of His grace. Let Him be the God of your desires and you will be drawn near to God and blessed.

3. Commit to an active prayer life:

If you are not consistently praying, your spiritual life will suffer. The Bible tells us to pray without ceasing (1 Thessalonians 5:17). Key ingredients to an active prayer life include setting aside a specific time for prayer each day. If you don't set a specific prayer time, you will not be consistent. For many people, getting up an hour early is a good habit. Take time to praise God for who He is. Acknowledge Him as God and acknowledge His right to lead your life. When struggles arise, acknowledge His sovereignty along with your petitions. Proverbs 3:6 tell us that if we acknowledge Him in all our ways, He will direct our paths.

Let Him direct you even when you can't see the end result. When you acknowledge Him as God, you will be more able to thank Him for what He has done and is doing. Thanksgiving is critical. Confess sins and keep short accounts with God. Also, intercede for others. God strengthens those who obey Him by praying for others.

4. Commit to changing your lifestyle:

When I was studying programming, the first thing we learned is the acronym "GIGO". It stands for "Garbage In, Garbage Out." If you put garbage into your mind, your spiritual life will be garbage as well. Your life cannot be contaminated with garbage and be spirit-filled at the same time. Not only must you renew your mind, but you must also guard your heart and mind from the world. Determine what is really of value in your life. Will you regret not watching MTV when you look back on your life? Does Jerry Springer add anything of value to your life? Weigh the worth of your movies, sitcoms, and other sources of influence. Sometimes we sacrifice what is truly valuable in exchange for what is truly worthless.

I am not trying to tell anyone how to live-that decision is the responsibility of each individual. I can only give reference to my life. I struggled to give up things in my life that I didn't feel were necessarily wrong, but there was great benefit in removing hindrances that ran counter to my value system. There was a time when I believed that I could pick the good and ignore the garbage, but I no longer feel that way. The battle of temptation is not lost at the point of temptation. It is won or lost at the time we decide whether we are going to make that first compromise or if we will stand firm and focus on God. The first temptation to compromise is the point where we set the direction for our life and determine which path we will take. It is an uphill battle. The stakes are high and our choice is critical. I believe that God puts the same choice before us that He gave Israel when they entered the promise land. Deuteronomy 11: 26-28 declares:

> Behold, I set before you this day a blessing and a curse; a blessing, if ye obey the commandments of the Lord, your God, which I command you this day: and a curse, if ye will not obey the commandments of the Lord your God, but turn aside out of the way which I command you this day, to go after other gods, which ye have not known.

We can make Him our God or we can make our desires god. A sinful lifestyle is a curse in itself. I lived by my desires before I knew Christ and I found no satisfaction. After I accepted Christ, I did not have direction and quickly went back to my old lifestyle. Once again, I pursued my own desires until one day I looked up and told God that I had no enjoyment in my life. For years, I struggled trying to break free of the curse of my sins and could not. Finally as a broken man, I began to seek the God who at the time seemed so distant. I did not give up and He delivered me from the chains that I could not break. Solomon said it best—he did not deny himself any pleasure but came to the conclusion that it was all vanity, empty and meaningless.

Pleasures outside of God's will always produce emptiness. Each choice of obedience gives me more fulfillment and more satisfaction. My prayer is that you commit to purity and trust God to be the One who fulfills your desires.

> The blessings of the Lord, it maketh rich,
> and he addeth no sorrow with it."
> —Proverbs 10:22

CHAPTER SIXTEEN

FLYING HIGH!

At two years old, Jonathan had his first flying experience, from Washington National Airport to St. Louis, Missouri. A year later he flew with us to Phoenix, Arizona and then in a small four-seat aircraft over the Grand Canyon. But it was not until he visited Andrews Air Force Base as a five-year-old that the flying bug bit him, and the desire to be a pilot grew stronger with each passing year.

By the time he was 16 the young man with the build of a swimmer and an easy smile had decided that flying jet fighters was his idea of heaven. He applied for entrance to the Air Force Academy. But we redirected our energetic son on a mission trip to New Zealand where he rekindled his love for God yet struggled with a dilemma that was resolved a year later when he decided he would be both a pilot and a missionary. On November 4, 2002, he completed his first solo flight.

Fellow student Tim Zajicek, was a sophomore when Jonathan moved into his dorm at Maranatha Bible College.

"Although he was a freshman he showed no reticence about walking up to me and introducing himself, and it didn't take long to realize we had the same love of flying. We both dreamed of being pilots! Our first conversation in the dorm hallway drew a lot of blank stares from other students as we indulged ourselves in using flying jargon that neither of us really understood. But soon we were taking flying lessons and our dreams were becoming real. We had the same flight instructor and we would argue about who was the better pilot as we swapped details of the exciting new things we were learning. On a flight to Sheybogan from Watertown some time later we jumped out of our plane after the short hop and threw a football around for a while. Then we just sat and talked about life. It seemed like the most natural thing to do. Jonathan was that kind of guy. Around him, even the most mundane things seemed to take on new meaning, and exceptional experiences became routine. I never remember him having a bad day.

"Like many others who knew him I asked a lot of questions about his passing away, and I've been able to answer only one-what if the Lord Jesus Christ never came to this earth to die on the cross for our sins so that we might have everlasting life? You and I would be bound for hell with no hope. But Christ did come; He forgives the sins of those who believe on Him; Jonathan believed on Him, so his sins were forgiven-and now he is present with the Lord. It is such a comfort to be assured that Jonathan knew the Lord Jesus as his personal Savior and at this very moment is standing in His presence. While you and I don't understand why things happen in life, we know that God makes no mistakes. His perfect plan saw fit to take Jonathan home. Though it is hard to grasp why God would take such a young man who was planning to serve Him with his life, we can take comfort in knowing that Jonathan was able to touch many lives in the short time he was here on earth. Even in the darkest, roughest moments of life, the name of our Lord Jesus can still be exalted.

"I know Jonathan's desire today would be that many would come to know Christ as a result of his passing away."

That prayer has been answered many times over. Through his death, Jonathan Leber is flying higher than even he could imagine. At the memorial service held for him at Maranatha Baptist College many acquaintances—particularly through his work as a swimming instructor—responded to an invitation to receive Jesus Christ as their Savior. And more than a dozen students surrendered their lives to full-time Christian service.

Back at his home church in Virginia the memorial service on May 4, 2005, drew a standing-room-only crowd of 2,000 people to hear him preach again the sermon he had delivered there only a few months before: "How Real Is Your God?"

CHAPTER SEVENTEEN

A DATE WITH ETERNITY

At the end of his first year of college, in May 2003, Jonathan had stayed over to complete his pilot license certification. He had finished the written and oral examination but still needed to perform his flight test. The weather was not cooperating so he drove home to Virginia. A few weeks later, he checked with the FAA instructor and was advised that the weather would be good for a few days so he drove back to Wisconsin where he passed his pilot examination without a hitch, on June 19. Now the only hurdle that remained was to complete the instrumentation course that would make him a fully fledged pilot licensed to fly in all conditions, day or night. This last step required many hours of cross-country flying and Jonathan would fly into Canada or to Michigan, New York and elsewhere to visit his friends. At times someone would accompany him and sometimes he would fly alone.

It was on the last leg of just such a cross country flight that he made his date with eternity. From our human perspective we would say that Jonathan had an accident, but from God's perspective, it was not so. In God's eyes, Jonathan's death was a well-planned event. The weather on the Friday at the start of that fateful weekend was clear and sunny, with the temperature nudging 70 degrees. By Sunday it had dropped to below freezing and there was snow in Michigan and Wisconsin. Looking back from a vantage point of a year later it is tempting to play the "If Only" game: If only I had not given him permission to fly that weekend; if only the college Dean had not signed his permission slip to leave the campus; if only his usual airplane had been available; if only he had a few minutes of gasoline left in the tank...

But as Christians we draw a circle around each "if only" and look instead to the providence of God, who is greater than all possibilities. His providential hand is upon our whole life, not just in the good times but in the bad times too. We use the word "accident" but God does not. He uses all kinds of events and means to bring His children home to glory. Our moment of death is according to His timetable. We cannot control events that are outside of us: all we are responsible for is how we react to those events as they unfold. In Jonathan's case, neither he nor any other human being knew ahead of time that the accident was going to happen that evening of April

25, 2005. We draw strength and peace from the certain knowledge that his death was not a random act of fate-on the contrary, he died under God's love and care. He could have died in bed that night but what better way to leave this earth than to go while doing what he loved best? He loved to fly and he loved to swim.

God is the Creator of this universe and the One who created us. He expressed His love for us by sending His Son to die for the sins of all mankind. Then to prove His deity, Jesus Christ was resurrected just three days later. So it is that our best example of how to face death in our final moments is to reflect on Christ, as I am sure Jonathan must have done. Jesus our Savior died willingly so we can die triumphantly!

But all of these thoughts were in the future on the morning of April 26, 2005, as I got ready for work. I called Jonathan's cell phone and left a message for him to call me and let me know that he was okay. No special prompting led me to do this-it was just the action of a mother caring for her son.

At 8:30 A.M. the Ohio Coast Guard called to advise my husband John that our son was missing. John asked about the weather conditions, the water temperature of the lake, and the air temperature at the time that the airplane went into Lake Michigan. The Coast Guard officer indicated that they were still searching, but there was no airplane wreckage or any trace of Jonathan. When his father spoke to me a few minutes later we both understood the implications of the stunning news: it would take a miracle to save our boy.

At 9:00 A.M. three television news vans arrived at our home, asking for interviews. Our hearts were breaking but we realized that what we said to the media could bring honor and glory to the Lord. Three separate interviews followed and that night they were featured on all the major news channels. Throughout the next days and couple of weeks, friends and relatives poured into the Leber home or telephoned to mourn and offer their condolences.

The aircraft was located on Thursday, April 28. Jerry Guyer, owner of Pirate's Cove Dive Company, traced the whereabouts of the single-engine Piper Archer by using coordinates of its last known radar signal and following them with the advanced sonar equipment on his boat. At noon, the sonar revealed what appeared to be the plane. On the following day Jerry Guyer dove alone into the 41 degree water and found the little aircraft nose-down on the bottom at about 160 feet. The plane's door was open and the cell phone lay next to it in the sand.

"Jonathan would not have survived long in those waters," Mr. Guyer said later. "After 17 minutes, protected by the best wetsuit and underwear that money can buy, I was already shivering cold."

Two months later he called to say that he had retrieved Jonathan's backpack from inside the airplane, and his cell phone. A box containing the backpack and phone arrived on June 21. Inside were Jonathan's clothes, his pocket Bible and his laptop computer and iPod. Besides his clothing, the only useable item worth saving was his Bible.

A few days later the aircraft was retrieved from the lakebed, floating gently to the surface after Jerry Guyer's crew dove to the bottom and attached air-filled lifting bags. Then a rope was tied from the company's boat to the propeller of the plane and it was dragged slowly to the Milwaukee shoreline where a crane lifted it from the water. The towing process took about three hours. The airplane sustained minimal damage.

CHAPTER EIGHTEEN

LIFE GOES ON

After the friends and relatives had gone home and the cards and notes stopped pouring in each day, life slowly returned to normal. Except that it could never be "normal" again. Our family—John, Kathy and Danielle—did not feel some supernatural presence or an overwhelming feeling of God's comfort, but we were aware of the many prayers for us that helped us to make it through those first difficult days.

Now God's grace sustains us. The fact is that even when we are hurting, others need us, so we keep on keeping on. Our purpose is to be helpful, to focus on the Lord and meet other people's needs. There are no easy answers to alleviate the pain of our loss, but God's Word proves true. King David wrote during his time of despair (Psalm 34:18-19):

*The Lord is nigh unto them that are of a broken
heart, and saveth such as be of a contrite spirit.
Many are the afflictions of the righteous: but the
Lord delivereth him out of them all.*

It still seems so strange to his father and me that
Jonathan is gone. We focused our lives on raising our
children so that they would turn out right and follow
the Lord's will, and now as we look back to the night
of the accident, it seems like a dream. Death is so final to those people still here on earth—it leaves us so
empty and alone. And it compels us to consider our
own mortality. Tragedy can strike at any time and
anywhere, knocking us off balance and leaving us
battered, emotionally scarred, shocked and stunned.
Then come the questions: How do I handle this loss?
How do I go on? Will I ever feel normal again? How
we react says a lot about us. Facing tragedy is not
a short- lived event, it is a life-long journey. I see
that now. And I'm grateful that I have my faith in
God to sustain me on that journey. Ultimately, my
relationship with Him is what matters most in this
life. Jesus tells us in John 16:33:

*These things I have spoken unto you, that in Me ye
might have peace.
In the world ye shall have tribulation: but be of good
cheer, I have overcome the world.*

These words are sobering and yet an encouragement. There is peace in the midst of the storm.
Christ paved the way for us. An athlete who excels

in a sport must face and overcome pain and injury. This is also true of life. No one goes unscathed. We endure by running the race that is set before us, looking constantly to the One who is the author and sustainer of our faith.

We're grateful to our Christian friends who understand the meaning of grief and are patient with our tears. We have discovered that the pain of grief is as deep as the joy of our love, and it is immensely comforting to know that we and our Christian friends all share an awareness of the depths of our Father's grief as He witnessed the death of His Son. Tears are a language God understands. Weeping is a built-in system to bath our emotions and is a release for our grief. Jesus wept over the death of His friend, Lazarus.

Death is real in a way that few other things are real. I have become more aware and more sensitive to the pain and suffering that people are going through when they lose a loved one. Also, I have learned to appreciate people more while they are still living. Thankfully, I have no regrets about my relationship with my son, Jonathan. He was a good son. He was a huge part of our lives and has left a huge hole in our hearts. Because we always gave our children so much love, time, and attention it is hard to focus beyond the void that is suddenly here, where Jonathan once was. Around me, I see children playing, people laughing; this one getting ready to graduate from college or that one getting engaged to be married. How do I get past the painful reality of Jonathan never doing these things? I do, because I must. And I can, because I am not alone!

It hurts to say good-bye. Sooner or later, though, the things we hold dear will all be taken from us. The parting may be gentle or hard, but is it always painful. Yet because this world is not my home, and I'm just passing through, I have an eternal perspective that makes all loss bearable, even the loss of my dear son. Something better is yet to come. Separation is only temporary.

About three weeks after Jonathan's death, I wrote a song to try to express the way I feel.

THE MASTER WEAVER

In Loving Memory of Jonathan D. Leber
By Kathy Leber—9 May, 2005

1. Though we have pain and loneliness, Our Savior truly knows.
    With loving arms, He surrounds us to lead us where to go.
    No trial is too great for Christ: He'll help us stand the test;
    He'll take the heavy burden now and give us peace and rest.

Chorus:
    God's ways are never wrong. His love is forever strong.

As the Master weaves the pattern He has planned,
We must trust the Master's hand,
For His view is from above
As He shows us, His great love.

2. Studying as a mission's pilot, God chose to take home Ace,
    For others now to take his place, as part of God's full plan.
    Our lives are finest tapestry fashioned by His care -
    Though we don't understand His ways, the threads are fine, and rare.

Chorus:
    God's ways are never wrong. His love is forever strong.
    As the Master weaves the pattern He has planned,
    We must trust the Master's hand,
    For His view is from above
    As He shows us, His great love.

3. A strand of sorrow may be there, though it's hard to perceive
    We must thank our Lord and Savior who knows our every need.
    When the loom is finally silent and shuttles cease to fly,

Our God will unroll the canvas and we'll know the reason why.

Chorus:
God's ways are never wrong. His love is forever strong.
As the Master weaves the pattern He has planned,
We must trust the Master's hand,
For His view is from above
As He shows us, His great love.

CHAPTER NINETEEN

LAST SERMONS

The last sermon Jonathan preached was not at his funeral; it lay in the miraculously preserved pages of his Bible recovered from the depths of Lake Michigan.

Opened under the tender hands of Jonathan's sister, Danielle, who painstakingly unglued the leather covers and then each sodden page, the Bible revealed a treasure trove of sermons and jotted thoughts.

Most startling was a folded piece of blue paper tucked into the back of the book. On one side was an outline of the so-called Romans Road collection of soul-winning scriptures, and on the other, written by Jonathan in blue ink, was the question, "How real is your God." Exposure to water had caused the ink to bleed through the paper and the adjacent white pages, but no ink had marred any portion of God's Word.

Other notes were found scattered throughout the Bible. They bear fitting testimony as the last words of a young man who tried so hard to live by them.

CHRISTIANS!

Should not be:
Whining, whimpering, wandering, wasting,
wavering, wearing or worrying!
Instead, we should be:
Worshiping, waiting, watching, working, warring,
warning, weeping, witnessing and winning!

**Lord, let me just be a NOBODY
Telling EVERYBODY
About SOMEBODY
Who can save ANYBODY.**

Remember-in labors of love, every day is pay day!

178

Psalm 137
God's
Redemption
At
Christ's
Expense

God Sent His Son To Be The Savior
If our greatest need had been knowledge
God would have sent His Son as an Educator.
If our greatest need had been money
God would have sent His Son as an Economist.
If our greatest need had been pleasure
God would have sent His Son as an
    Entertainer.
But our greatest need is salvation
So God sent His Son to be the Savior.
Is He your Savior?

Our talents and our possessions
We dare not ever hoard
But share them with real gratitude
AS UNTO CHRIST, OUR LORD.

Faith honors God. God honors faith.

BIBLE VERSES FOR YOU:
- I am a sinner. Romans 3:23.
- I deserve hell. Romans 6:23.
- God gave His Son. Romans 5:8
- I can be saved! Romans 10:9,10,13
- Can I know I'm saved? Yes! John 5:13.
- How long will I be saved? Forever! John 5:24; 10:28.
- What should I do when I sin? Get forgiveness!
                    I John 1:9.

It Works This Way
The more you give, the more you get;
The more you laugh, the less you fret;
The more you do unselfishly,
The more you live abundantly;
The more of everything you share,
The more you'll always have to spare;
The more you love, the more you'll find

That life is good and friends are
For only what you give away
Enriches you from day to day.

Today is here! Use it to God's Glory!

Commit To Change
James 3:11-12

Garbage In, Garbage Out! If you put garbage into your mind, your spiritual life will be garbage as well. Does a spring send forth fresh water and bitter from the same opening? You life cannot be contaminated with garbage and be Spirit-filled at the same time. Not only must you renew your mind, but you must also guard your heart and mind from the world. Determine what is really of value in your life. Will you regret not watching MTV when you look back on your life? Does Jerry Springer add anything of value to your life? What types of movies do you watch? How do you spend your time? Sometimes we sacrifice what is truly valuable in exchange for what is truly worthless.

Day By Day

Finish the day, and forget it.

Mistakes have crept in. Learn from them and leave them.

Once the night closes the door to the day, let it stay closed.

Tomorrow is a new day.

Begin with the Savior and the Scriptures.

Be fervent in your prayers,

Fearless in your principles,

Firm in your purposes,

Faithful in your promises.

Waste none of the day's hours.

Miss none of its opportunities.

Soil none of its moments.

Do your best, not your bit!

Eighteen inches can mean eternity with Christ
or an eternity without Christ.
Are your sure of your personal
relationship with Him?
Why not move the question from
your head to your heart and settle
it once and for all, right now?

The ideas Jonathan chose to carry about with him in his Bible underline his focus on others. Clearly, he believed there are two types of people in the world—those who come into a room and say "Here I am!" and those who come in and say, "There you are!" One approach demands attention and the other allows others to speak. One says "I'm important and the world revolves around me," and the other says, "I'm here to serve you." The second person is one that others love to be around.

God's Word provides practical advice on becoming a person who demonstrates Christ-likeness. We are to give preference to one another (Romans 12:10), build one another up (Romans 14:19); bear one another's burdens (Galatians 6:2), forgive one another (Colossians 3:13), care for one another (1 Corinthians 12:25), serve one another (Galatians 5:13), comfort one another (1 Thessalonians 5:11), and pray for one another (James 5:16). People with a heart for God have a heart for people!

Several complete sermons were also discovered in Jonathan's Bible. Fittingly, they speak of reaching out to the lost.

The Lost Son

And he said, A certain man had two sons: and the younger of them said to his father, Father, give me the portion of goods that falleth to me.

And he divided unto them his living.

And not many days after the younger son gathered all together, and took his journey into a far country, and there wasted his substance with riotous living.

And when he had spent all, there arose a mighty famine in that land; and he began to be in want.

And he went and joined himself to a citizen of that country; and he sent him into his fields to feed swine.

And he would fain have filled his belly with the husks that the swine did eat: and no man gave unto him.

And when he came to himself, he said, How many hired servants of my father's have bread enough and to spare, and I perish with hunger! I will arise and go to my father, and will say unto him, Father, I have sinned against heaven, and before thee, and am no more worthy to be called thy son: make me as one of thy hired servants.

And he arose, and came to his father.

But when he was yet a great way off, his father saw him, and had compassion, and ran, and fell on his neck, and kissed him.

And the son said unto him, Father, I have sinned against heaven, and in thy sight, and am no more worthy to be called thy son.

*But the father said to his servants, Bring forth the
best robe, and put it on him; and put a ring on his
hand, and shoes on his feet: And bring hither the
fatted calf, and kill it; and let us eat, and be merry:
For this my son was dead, and is alive again; he was
lost, and is found. And they began to be merry.*
—Luke 15:11-24

Jenny was a bright-eyed, pretty five-year-old girl.
One day when she and her mother were checking
out at the grocery store, Jenny saw a plastic pearl
necklace priced at $2.50. How she wanted that neck-
lace, and when she asked her mother if she would
buy it for her, her mother said, 'Well, it is a pretty
necklace, but it costs an awful lot of money. I'll tell
you what. I'll buy you the necklace, and when we
get home, we can make up a list of chores that you
can do to pay for the necklace. Don't forget that for
your birthday, Grandma just might give you a whole
dollar bill, too. Okay?' Jenny agreed, and her mother
bought the pearl necklace for her.

Jenny worked on her chores very hard every
day, and sure enough, her grandma gave her a brand
new dollar bill for her birthday. Soon Jenny had
paid off the pearls. How Jenny loved those pearls.
She wore them everywhere to kindergarten, to bed,
and when she sent out with her mother to run er-
rands. The only time she didn't wear them was in
the shower–her mother had told her that they would
turn her neck green!

This is somewhat the way of the younger son in this parable. He went and asked his father for his portion of the inheritance. By doing this, he created a series of events that I believe illustrate a lost person coming to Christ.

I.   He was Separated by sin from God.

A.   Sin is coming short of God's Glory.

Sin separates us from God's Glory. Paul wrote in Romans 3:23, *'For all have sinned, and come short of the glory of God.'*

A group of men needed to cross a gulf that was 30 feet across and more than 500 feet deep. The only way to cross this great chasm was by jumping. Some could jump 15 feet and others as far as 20 feet. A man once jumped 29 feet, 2 ½ inches at the 1968 Olympic Games, but this jump would still come short. All would come short; all have the same destiny. This is how you are today if you do not know Christ as your Lord and Savior. You come short of God's glory and therefore you are destined for Hell.

B.   Sin is Separation from God Eternally.

In the parable in Luke 15, the rich man was destined to burn eternally in hell for his sin. Romans 6:23 reads *'For the wages of sin is death, but the gift of God is eternal life through Jesus Christ our Lord.'*

The payment for sin is death. Sin is complete separation from God eternally.

II. He had a Realization of his Sin

A. Sin is frustration.

Paul wrote in Romans 7:24, *'O wretched man that I am! Who shall deliver me from the body of this death?'*

Even though Paul was saved, he knew that without Christ, life was confusing and meaningless. With God, we are comforted in times of trial. Sin causes frustration.

B. Sin is filth.

We see in Isaiah 64:6 that, *'...we are all as an unclean thing, and all our righteousness are as filthy rags; and we all do fade as a leaf; and our iniquities, like the wind, have taken us away.'*

If you are unsaved everything you do is, 'as filthy rags.' Salvation is not of works but by the grace of God as the Bible tells us in Ephesians 2:8-9. *'For by grace are ye saved through faith; and that not of yourselves: it is the gift of God: not of works, lest any man should boast.'*

If you are unsaved, everything you do is rejected by God, for you are filthier than the slop the pigs play in. You are unclean.

C. Sin is Death.

Paul wrote, *'For the wages of sin is death,'* in Romans 6:23a.

Sin has a penalty. That penalty is death. If you are unsaved, you will spend eternity in the Lake of Fire. Hell is the second death, as we see in

Revelation 20:15 *'And whosoever was not found written in the book of life was cast into the lake of fire.'*

An unbeliever is destined for the Lake of Fire for all eternity.

III. True Justification
True justification or true salvation is two-fold:

    A. It Includes Repentance:
        1. Intellectually, repentance is a change of view toward one's past actions. Acts 2:37-38 reads *'Now when they heard this, they were pricked in their heart, and said unto Peter and to the rest of the apostles, Men and brethren, what shall we do? Then Peter said unto them, Repent, and be baptized every one of you in the name of Jesus Christ for the remission of sins, and ye shall receive the gift of the Holy Ghost.'*
           The people knew they were sinners, they knew they were destined for Hell. They wanted to change.
        2. Emotionally, repentance is a genuine sorrow for sin given by God, a desire for pardon. 2 Corinthians 7:9-10 reads, *'Now I rejoice, not that ye were made sorry, but that ye sorrowed to repentance: for ye were made sorry after a godly manner, that ye might receive damage by us in nothing. For godly*

sorrow worketh repentance to salvation not to be repented of: but the sorrow of the world worketh death.'

Paul is saying that the peoples sorrow was of God, and that sorrow brought them to repentance. For true repentance, it must be from God.

3. Volitionally, repentance is a change of will. Proverbs 28:13 reads, *'He that covereth his sins shall not prosper: but whoso confesseth and forsaketh them shall have mercy.'*

Solomon tells us that true repentance from God changes our goals. Our will for our lives will become God's will.

B. It Includes Faith:

1. Faith has a sound basis. The author of Hebrews wrote in Hebrews 11:1, *'Now faith is the substance of things hoped for, the evidence of things not seen.'*

Our faith is based on substance, on the evidence of the eternal Word of God. To be saved, you put your complete trust in Jesus Christ to get you to heaven.

2. Faith is the Work of God. Faith does not include works.

Ephesians 2:8-9 reads *'For by grace are ye saved through faith; and that not of yourselves: it is the gift of God: not of works, lest any man should boast.'*

Faith is a gift of God's grace. Why then, if faith is a work of God, are we responsible for not having it? God wills to work faith in all. God is waiting for you to trust in Him, so that His Holy Spirit can create that faith in you. True justification, true salvation comes only from God.

For by grace are ye saved through faith; and that not of yourselves: it is the gift of God.'

God gives you the faith.

Now Jenny had a very loving daddy. When Jenny went to bed, he would get up from his favorite chair every night and read her favorite story. One night when he finished the story, he said, 'Jenny, do you love me?'

'Oh yes, Daddy, you know I love you,' the little girl said.

'Well, then, give me your pearls.'

'Oh! Daddy, not my pearls!' Jenny said. 'You can have Rosie, my favorite doll. Remember her? You gave her to me last year for my birthday. And you can have her tea party outfit, too. Okay?'

'Oh no, darling, that's okay. I won't take anything.' Her father brushed her cheek with a kiss. 'Good night, little one.'

A week later, her father once again asked Jenny after her story, 'Do you love me?'

She replied, 'Oh yes, Daddy, you know I love you.'

'Well, then, give me your pearls.'

'Oh, Daddy, not my pearls! But you can have Ribbons, my toy horse. Do you remember her? She's my favorite. Her hair is so soft, and you can play with it and braid it. You can have Ribbons if you want her, Daddy,' the little girl said to her father.

'No, I won't take anything;' her father said and brushed her cheek again with a kiss. Then he added, 'God bless you, little one. Sweet dreams.'

Several days later, when Jenny's father came in to read her a story, Jenny was sitting on her bed and her lip was trembling. 'Here Daddy,' she said and held out her hand. It held her beloved pearl necklace. She let it slip into her father's hand. He took the plastic pearls and with his other hand he pulled out of his pocket a blue velvet box. Inside the box were genuine, beautiful pearls. He had them all along, but he was waiting for Jenny to give up the cheap stuff so he could give her the real thing.

So it is with God. He is waiting for us to give up our unclean, filthy lives so He can give us His great gift of grace-salvation. God is waiting for you to say, 'Lord, I believe that you are God, and only by you can I experience true life. Forgive me of my sin so that I may know you.'

Please, if you are unsaved; do not put off this great offer. God loves you, and wants what is best for you. Please do not reject this gift one more second.

True Love
Mark 12:30-31

And thou shalt love the Lord thy God with all thy heart, and with all thy soul, and with all thy mind, and with all thy strength: this is the first commandment.
And the second is like, namely this, Thou shalt love thy neighbour as thyself.
There is none other commandment greater than these.

Do you truly love God?

In this passage Jesus repeats the idea expressed in Leviticus 19:18, that if we love God we will show it by loving our neighbor. Christians need to learn how to truly love God. Within verses 30 and 31, we see two points dealing with true love for God. First we see this:

I.   **The Way to love God**

    A. We need to love God with all our heart: The heart is the center of all physical and spiritual life.

        1. It's the vigor and sense of physical life.
Leviticus 17:11 reads, *'For the life of the flesh is in the blood...'*

192

The heart is the major muscle that pushes blood through our bodies. A human heart beats an average of 72 times a minute, forty million times a year, and two and a half billion times in a life of 70 years. Each beat the heart takes, 4 ounces of blood is discharged. This amounts to three thousand gallons a day. The heart does enough work in one hour to lift a 150 pound man to the top of a three-story building, enough energy in twelve hours to lift a 65 ton truck one-foot off the ground. Now that's a major muscle.

2. It's the center and seat of spiritual life.

The heart is the character of an individual. It tells us who the person really is and who or what that person cares about and what he believes. Paul wrote in Romans 10:10, *'For with the heart man believeth unto righteousness…'*

God died for us and that is cause enough for us to love God with all our hearts. By putting our faith in Christ to get us to heaven we show our love for God. God loved us so much that He gave His only Son to die for us. That alone deserves our love.

B. We need to love God with all our soul:

The soul is the seat of the sentient element in man; what we perceive, reflect, feel, and desire. This is our self-conscious life.

David wrote in Psalms 84:2,

My soul longeth, and even fainteth for the courts of the LORD...

Isaiah 26:9 reads,

With my soul have I desired thee in the night...

Our emotions need to be centered on our love for God. It is like when a man has strong feelings for a woman, he becomes self-conscious around her and she becomes nervous! He does not know what to say, he has a million things going through his mind at once. The girl becomes a main part of his feelings. That is the way God should be in our lives. All our wants and feelings should be centered around our love for God.

C. We need to love God with all our mind:

This is our thought capacity, our understanding, and our knowledge. God has given us understanding. Luke 24:45 reads, *Then he opened their understanding, that they might understand the Scriptures.*

Everything we learn about God should be for one purpose, because we love God. If we truly love God when we read and study God's Word, our minds will be set on what God wants from us and what He wants us to do.

D. We need to love God with all our strength: This is our ability, our might, and our power. 1 Peter 4:11 reads,...*let him do it as of the ability which God giveth...*

All we can do should be expressed in our love for God, because He gave us the ability to do it.

In August of 1973, eight year old Samantha White of Steilacoon, Washington, climbed to the top of 19,320-foot Mount Kilimanjaro.

She is believed to be the youngest person ever to conquer Africa's highest mountain. Her father, a United States airman, dropped out at 18,640 feet with altitude sickness. But this girl had a goal. She knew that she had a talent and was able to accomplish something great. This is how our love for God should be. All our talents and gifts come from God, and we should use them to honor and glorify God. Our ability, our might, and our power should show our love for God.

II. **The Result of a love for God:**
The ultimate result of having a love for God is a love for your neighbor, whether it be a friend or a foe. Paul wrote in Romans 15:2, *Let everyone of us please his neighbor for his good to edification.*

Also, in 1 Thessalonians 3:12, we read, *And the Lord make you to increase and abound in love one toward another, and toward all men,even as we do toward you.*

Jesus said in Matthew 5:44, *But I say unto you, Love your enemies, bless them that curse you, do good to them that hate you, and pray for them which despitefully use you, and persecute you.*
There is a story told about two young men, in the First World War, who had been friends for their entire lifetime. Being neighbors, they had played together, gone to school together, engaged in the same athletic programs, and finally had enlisted in the army together. Fate determined they would eventually be in the same area of battle together. After a particularly hard battle one day, it was found that one of the boys was missing somewhere

out in what is known as 'No Man's Land.'
The other boy, safe and unhurt, went to the
commanding officer and requested permission to go out and look for his friend. He
was told it was of no use for no one was alive
out there after the withering fire of so many
hours. After great insistence, he was finally
given permission to go. Sometime later, he
came with the limp body of his friend over
his shoulder.

The commander said, "Didn't I tell you it was
no use to go?"

The boy replied with radiance in his eyes,
"But it was not wasted. I got there in time to
hear him whisper, 'I knew you'd come.'"

God has made love the most important thing
in life. *'Love is the fulfilling of the law'* according to Romans 13:8-10. If we truly love God,
His love will indwell us, and it will in turn be
reflected to others. We do not love by rules
but by a relationship with God that in turn
enables us to have a loving relationship with
others.

So, do you truly love God?

CHAPTER TWENTY

STILL PREACHING!

Life is not fair. But every unfair, contrary, unexpected or difficult circumstance is an opportunity in disguise! God is able to use every challenge we face as an opportunity to reveal His glory. As long as there is sin in the world, life will not be fair, but if we just take our eyes off ourselves for a moment we will discover a true perspective on life. What, after all, could be more unfair then Jesus Christ, the Sinless One, taking our sins and punishment upon Himself?

So Jonathan's death is hard to reconcile with the promise of his life, but not hard to reconcile with the promise of God found in John 12:24 -

Except a corn of wheat fall into the ground and die, it abideth alone: but if it die it bringeth forth much fruit.

Jonathan's death has already borne much fruit, and will continue to do so. He is gone, but the memory of him is still preaching, as are the words he left behind.

Billy Buchholtz wrote an essay for his public school to commemorate his swim coach, Jon Leber.

"He was my best friend, my role model, and my swimming coach for the past three years of my life. He was the assistant coach of the Watertown Boys Swim Team. His Christian, carefree attitude glowed as he walked across the deck to talk with us about school, swimming, or life in general.

"On April 26, 2005, all the members of the boy's swim team were called to the main office of our high school. A police officer entered and a serious mood sank deep into my chest. He told us that Coach Jon was flying his single engine plane over Lake Michigan and ran out of fuel. His plane landed in the icy water where he survived the crash, called 911 and attempted to swim to shore. Unfortunately, the extremely low water temperatures made it virtually impossible for Jon to reach shore. Jon was a highly conditioned and competitive swimmer so I was not going to give up hope. However, weeks passed and hope was lost. Our swim team suffered an immeasurable loss.

"Looking back, Jon helped sculpt who I am as an individual. Not only did he want us to succeed in the water but also in academics. Through his coaching I did thrive in both of these aspects. By swimming in the state meet and remaining on the high honor roll throughout my high school career, I fulfilled Jon's aspirations. However, without him as our team motivator I had to step into the spotlight. Because of this I became determined to succeed in swimming, helping others and reflecting Jon's Christian beliefs. Though there is room for me to grow, I am determined to carry these life-pursuing attributes with me to overcome any obstacles. There was more to life than just swimming for Jon, and he taught me how to succeed through hard work, self-motivation and kindness to others."

Areobaldo deCarvalho, a missionary to Africa was visiting churches to raise support. On May 21, 2005, he shared Jonathan's story during his time of preaching and five people were saved.

Daniel Perez, a high school friend, heard the news of Jonathan's death in Navy boot camp. He shared the story with his bunkmate and led the young man to salvation.

In a letter to Jonathan's mother he declared: "That was probably the highlight of boot camp for me!"

Kip Tatusko, a Youth Pastor, wrote to say that Jonathan was still changing lives.

"Last month I took the teen group in my church on their annual ski retreat. I focused on the need to

'Choose Christ Now', encouraging them to make their faith in Christ an active, everyday relationship, and not to sit back passively and expect God to respond. Jonathan's sermon 'How real is your God?' came immediately to mind as I put together ideas and activities for the retreat.

"I decided to play only Jonathan's sermon from the memorial DVD, not informing the teens beforehand about any of Jonathan's story except that I knew him from FBT and he was an exceptional young man. I didn't need to say much because I knew his words and disposition would speak for itself. I knew Jonathan could relate to the teens, who would see him as someone they might have for a friend.

"After hearing the sermon, the teens were overwhelmingly impressed with Jonathan's conviction and fervor. They were surprised that someone so bright, athletic, well-spoken and popular would have the desire for Christ that Jonathan showed. Often young men like Jonathan get easily distracted by the other opportunities a life of that nature would present, yet Jonathan exhibited such a heart-felt desire for Christ.

"Needless to say, the teens were absolutely floored when I told them of the plane crash. Mostly, they were speechless. Not because of the apparent tragedy but because more than ever they were hit by the immediacy of his message. Every teen in the room, maybe for the first time, deeply considered whether God was a distant, *surreal* being or truly a *real*, intimate God and Father. There is no question in my mind that Jonathan's sermon will have a long-lasting impact on the teens. All because Jonathan was bold enough to hold his love for God closer than anything else in life. If they had never asked the question before, it now resonates in their heads and hearts: How real is my God?

Alan Bolds, the director of Vision Teams for Awana Clubs International wrote to say that he was planning to publish Jonathan's story on the Awana Website the week of April 24, 2006, to commemorate the one-year anniversary of his home-going.

"Awana's Website is viewed by thousands of people every month and I know that people will be touched by Jonathan's devotion to the Lord. Thank you for allowing us to share his story with the Awana family worldwide."

Jonathan Leber made an impact on others by his life and by his death not because he was perfect but because he lived as he died—pursuing his convictions. The legacy of such a life will inevitably endure.

Speaking of Christians and their convictions, he wrote, "We need to set up our own convictions and guidelines. We should not just follow someone else's convictions, we need to think for ourselves and make our own convictions and guidelines. We need to build our lives on strong foundations that are rooted in the Bible. Take time to understand and study the Bible, seeking for good foundation in your life. Be discerning when setting up convictions, scrutinize the evidence."

His modified version of the well-known KISS principle used by speech coaches (Keep It Simple, Stupid) was, Keep It Strictly Scriptural!

One of his favorite verses was Ecclesiastes 12:13-

> *Let us hear the conclusion of the whole matter:*
> *Fear God, and keep his commandments:*
> *for this is the whole duty of man.*

This fervent sense of conviction was translated into preaching in which he challenged his audience to do more and be more for God. Such messages live on in the minds and hearts of those who heard him speak.

TAKE THAT STAND
Acts 16:16-40

Are you willing to take a stand for the Gospel? Paul and Silas were willing to take a stand. They were beaten and thrown into prison, but still rejoiced through their persecution. From that, great opportunities arose. The Bible tells us to run the race with patience, press toward the mark, and keep the faith. We, as Christians, need to stand up for the truth of the Gospel for we are the bearers of the light for this cold, dark world.

In this passage, we first see:

I. **The Stand (verses 16-18)**

We see no reason why this demon-possessed girl was following Paul and Silas around for so many days, but the entire time that she was doing so she cried, "These men are the servants of the most high God!" Satan and his demons know a great deal about God and the Scriptures. Every time demons met Jesus, they immediately recognized Him as the Son of God.

A. In Matthew 8:29, the demon-possessed men at Gadara asked:
   What have we to do with thee, Jesus, thou Son of God?

B. In Mark 1:24, the man in Capernaum with the unclean spirit cried,
   Let us alone; what have we to do with thee, thou Jesus of Nazareth?
   Art thou come to destroy us?
   I know thee who thou art, the Holy One of God.

C. Also, in Mark 3:11, the unclean spirits cried,
   Thou art the Son of God.

So the demon possessing this girl recognized Paul and Silas as men of God. It could be the demon wanted to gain more popularity by telling who Paul and Silas were, but mainly the devil was using the woman as a dangerous tool against the Church. When the devil tells the truth about the Bible, about Jesus, or about believers, it makes the church vulnerable to false doctrine and false teachers. Paul knew this and rebuked the girl's testimony, and cast the demon out. Paul stood firm for the faith and the church.

We need Pastors, Missionaries, and local church members who will follow Paul's example; men and women who will stand up for God and His local church. If we let religions deny the virgin birth and the verbal inspiration of the Scriptures, and deny the fact that God sent His only Son to die on Calvary's tree and shed His blood for your sins and mine; these false teachings will destroy local churches all across this globe.

God's Word commands us in 2 Corinthians 6:14,

> *Be ye not unequally yoked together with unbelievers: for what fellowship hath righteousness with unrighteousness?*
> *And what communion hath light with darkness?'*

A passage in II John and verses 7 through 11 takes this thought even further:

> *For many deceivers have gone out into the world who do not confess Jesus Christ as coming in the flesh.*
> *This is a deceiver and an antichrist.*

Look to yourselves, that we do not lose those things which we have wrought, but that we receive a full reward.

Whosoever transgresseth, and abideth not in the doctrine of Christ hath not God.

He that abideth in the doctrine of Christ, he hath both the Father and the Son.

If there come any unto you, and bring not this doctrine, receive him not into your house, neither bid him God speed: for he that biddeth him God speed is partaker of his evil deeds.'

So you see there are religions in this world that Satan is using to destroy the local church and to subdue the spread of the Gospel of Christ. This passage tells us that they are deceivers and Christ commands never to let them into your house and never, ever wish them God speed, for if you do, you will be guilty of the same evil deeds. This includes Jehovah witnesses, Mormons, Roman Catholics, Universalists, Hindus, Buddhists, Muslims, and I could go on and on but I won't for times sake. Don't take this in a way that I mean to hate them (for we are commanded to love them), but do not be overtaken by their false doctrine and teachings.

II. **The Persecution for Standing (verses 19-25)**

When you stand up for the faith, people notice, and when people notice, persecution most likely will erupt. For centuries, we see Christians being persecuted for the Gospel.

From the day Christ came, to the present, and even those who had faith in God before Christ came to this earth, were persecuted for their faith.

A. **Paul and Silas Were Beaten** (verses 19-24).
   They were beaten for standing for Christ. Verses 22 and 23 read:

And the multitude rose up together against them: and the magistrates rent off their clothes, and commanded to beat them.
And when they had laid many stripes upon them, they cast them into prison, charging the jailor to keep them safely.

Now here in the US, we are not beaten with rods and thrown into prison for standing strong in the faith, but we are beaten verbally or shunned. There is only one thing that I think is worse than being thrown in prison for standing up for what is right, and that is being persecuted by your own brethren in the faith. I tell you, I would rather be in prison for my faith than be shunned by a fellow believer because he is not willing to take a stand.

B. **Paul and Silas Rejoiced through the persecution** (verse 25).
   Look at their reaction to their persecution-they sang and prayed unto God. We must remember that even though we feel

all alone God is there with you carrying you. There is a story by Mary Stevenson Parker called "**Footprints.**"

One night a man had a dream. He dreamed he was walking along the beach with the LORD. Across the sky flashed scenes from his life. For each scene, he noticed two sets of footprints in the sand; one belonged to him, and the other to the LORD.

When the last scene of his life flashed before him, he looked back at the footprints in the sand. He noticed that many times along the path of his life there was only one set of footprints. He also noticed that it happened at the very lowest and saddest times in his life.

This really bothered him and he questioned the LORD about it. "LORD, you said that once I decided to follow you, you'd walk with me all the way. But I have noticed that during the most troublesome times in my life, there is only one set of footprints. I don't understand why when I needed you most you would leave me."

The LORD replied, "My precious, precious child, I love you and I would never leave you. During your times of trial and suffering, when you see only one set of footprints, it was then that I carried you."

God has promised that He will never leave us nor forsake us and therefore, we can rejoice in persecution. Look at Matthew 5:11 and 12:

Blessed are ye, when men shall revile you, and persecute you, and shall say all manner of evil against you falsely, for my sake.

Rejoice, and be exceeding glad: for great is your reward in heaven: for so persecuted they the prophets which were before you.

Paul and Silas could have easily blamed God for what happened, but they did not and it created some awesome results.

III. The Results of Standing and Rejoicing (versus 26-40).

A. People come to Christ (versus 26-29): Because Paul and Silas rejoiced during their persecution, the jailor noticed. Look at verses 26-29:

And suddenly there was a great earthquake, so that the foundations of the prison were shaken: and immediately all the doors were opened, and every one's bands were loosed.
And the keeper of the prison awaking out of his sleep, and seeing the prison doors open, he drew out his sword, and would have killed himself, supposing that the prisoners had been fled.
But Paul cried with a loud voice, saying, Do thyself no harm: for we are all here.
Then he called for a light, and sprang in, and came trembling, and fell down before Paul and Silas.

Remember people do notice when you take a stand. When Paul and Silas prayed and sang, God did a mighty work that night.

There was an earthquake, the jail doors flew open, and just as the jailer was about to kill himself, Paul and Silas said, wait we are still here. Then the jailer ran in and knew these men were of the true and living God and asked, 'What must I do to be saved?' And that night the jailer and his family were saved. So, people do notice when you take a stand and rejoice through persecution. This jailer sure did.

B. Creates a Stronger Testimony (versus 35-40)

When you take a stand and rejoice, your own people will notice. When people see that you are wanting to do what is right, they will see the joy and blessings in your life and will wonder, "How can they be so happy and yet be under such stress from this persecution?" When you take a stand people will notice and it will create a stronger testimony on your part and eventually people will want to follow your lead.

So my challenge to born-again, Bible believing Christians is that you take a stand for what you know is right. Satan is out to destroy the local church to keep the Gospel from spreading. Don't believe Satan's lies, because when it sounds good there is always a catch. May God be able to say, "Well done thou good and faithful servant."

Fight the good fight of faith starting today. Let's take a stand for the Gospel. As a believer, you are to serve Jesus and others, not self. Remember the word, JOY means Jesus, Others, and You which means me or myself last. Our Lord Jesus said in Matthew 20:26-28,

> *It shall not be so among you: but whosoever will be great among you, let him be your minister; and whosoever will be chief among you, let him be your servant: Even as the Son of man came not to be ministered unto, but to minister, and to give his life a ransom for many.*

Our Master and Savior, Jesus is our example. He came not to be served but to serve and give His life on the cross for the sin of the world that we may have eternal life with Him for all eternity. True greatness is not measured by giving orders but by serving. God measures greatness by our service to Him. Obeying God brings purpose to life. When you do not know what to do, turn to the Bible for the answers for every day living. For the Bible is the believer's final authority. The Bible stands for:

Basic
Instructions
Before
Leaving
Earth

God's people are to be servers. No service for the Lord whether great or small should be done grudgingly. It should be a privilege to serve Christ. So do it with gladness in your heart. Look forward to doing what God has called you to do and do it with a joyful heart and an attitude of gratitude. Also, serve the Lord willingly. Serve Him with your whole heart. It should be something we want to do because of what Christ did for us. Be a sold-out 24-hour Christian serving Him wholeheartedly. Ephesians 6:7 tell us to do "service as to the Lord, and not to men."

To get the most out of life, make every second count for God. Keep trying, struggling, and asking God for His wisdom, strength, and guidance to do His Will. None of us knows how many days we have left on this earth. Each day is a gift from God-that is why it is called "the present." Christian, please don't waste it. The conversion of the soul is a miracle from God of the moment, but the growth of a saint is a task that takes a lifetime. What God does through you here is of value for all eternity. Serve Him sacrificially and it will be rewarded by the Lord Himself.

David Livingstone said, "He is the greatest Master I have ever known. If there is anyone greater, I do not know of him. Jesus Christ is the only Master supremely worthy of serving. He is the only ideal that never loses its inspiration. He is the only friend whose friendship meets every demand. He is the only Savior who can save to the uttermost. We go forth in His Name, in His power, and in His Spirit to serve Him."

Civilizations and nations will fall but the human soul lives forever. Someday, every individual will stand and face God's judgment. Hebrews 9:27-28 states:

And as it is appointed unto men once to die, but after this the judgment: so Christ was once offered to bear the sins of many; and unto them that look for him shall he appear the second time without sin unto salvation.

Will we have indescribable joy or will we be exiled from God forever? What an awesome responsibility the believer has! We must tell people that the only way to eternity with God is to accept Christ's offer of forgiveness and reconciliation. John 5:24 reads:

Verily, verily, I say unto you, He that heareth my word, and believeth on him that sent me, hath everlasting life, and shall not come into condemnation; but is passed from death unto life.

Only through God's grace do we have life eternal with Jesus. The best investment is a wise and permanent investment. If we are wise, we will be preparing for what lasts forever. Things seen are temporal but things not seen are eternal. Are you so absorbed with your own interests and pleasures that you forget the countless scores of people who are stumbling blindly toward hell? Warn these people of the urgency of accepting Jesus into their hearts today. Be a messenger that delivers the good news of Jesus Christ. Colossians 1:28 commands:

Him we preach, warning every man and teaching every man in all wisdom, that we may present every man perfect, in Christ Jesus.

Don't wait, for tomorrow may never come. What is life about? It is preparation for eternity. Eventually, this world and all that we have accumulated will someday burn up. Are you ready for your final destination of life beyond the grave?

CHAPTER TWENTY ONE

FINAL DESTINATION

Where will you spend eternity if you were to die suddenly like Jonathan Leber did? Would you wake up in the presence of God who created each one of us? Is there any hesitation in your answer?

You may question if there really is life after death. If I live my life as if there really is an eternity to follow, and I'm wrong, what have I lost? But if you live as if there is no tomorrow, and *you're* wrong, you have lost everything! You face an eternity in hell. If you don't have an absolute assurance that you are going to heaven, there's a good chance that you are not. Is it worth the risk, to continue for one more moment unsure of where you will spend eternity? Would you want to escape hell if you could? Is there somebody you know or love who you would turn from hell, if you could?

The fact is, you can know with absolute assurance that heaven is your final destination. The first thing to understand is that heaven is not a reward and hell is not a punishment—they are actual places. Next, you must understand that you do not have to be good to go to heaven but you must be perfect! That's God's standard. Of course, neither you nor I are perfect—Jesus Christ is the only perfect man who ever walked this earth. And God loves us so much that His perfect Son was put to death in our place, to trade His perfection for our imperfection. He died on the cross for all the sins of the world, and offers you and me the free gift of an eternal life in heaven that can only be enjoyed by perfect people. We cannot earn this gift. We don't deserve it. All we can do is accept it, with gratitude.

What do you have to lose by accepting this gift? Nothing but hell. In the New Testament, Jesus Christ is recorded as telling a story that graphically illustrates the reality and the horror of hell. Luke 16:19-31 briefly describes the experiences of two men, one in hell and one in heaven, and highlights the awful suffering of the man in hell who begs for just one drop of water. "Have mercy on me!" he cries, "for I am tormented in this flame."

Christ was warning us in this story that our eternal destiny after we die is irrevocable. There is no turning back. This is why we must be sure of our destiny now, today, because nobody knows how much time we have on this earth. Life is very fragile. It can be snuffed out in full stride. Yet it is true for the Christian that departure from this life provides entrance into a more glorious life that is imperishable and eternal.

A professor once tried to communicate the essence of the gospel to the students in his class. Most of the students refused to take his course seriously. Finally, the professor asked one of his best students who was studying for the ministry to stay after class so he could talk to him. The professor knew that in addition to his flawless GPA the student was also an accomplished athlete and he wondered how many push-ups he could do. The student, JD, replied that he did 200 push-ups each night. The professor asked him if he could do 300 in sets of ten. JD thought he could, so he was told to come to class early the next day and sit in the front of the room. When the class began, the professor placed a big box of doughnuts on his table. It was the last day before the weekend and everybody was excited to get the class over with.

The professor asked Jenny, on the front row, "Do you want one of these doughnuts?" She said, "Yes!" Then the professor turned to JD and asked him to do ten push-ups so Jenny could have a doughnut. When the push-ups were completed the professor handed Jenny her doughnut.

Then the professor went to the next student, Sue, and asked her if she wanted a doughnut. Her response was also an enthusiastic "Yes!" Again, JD completed ten push-ups for Sue and she got her doughnut. Each person on that row was asked the same question in turn, and JD did ten push-ups for each of them. He finished the first and second rows, but when the professor got to the third row and asked Nate if he wanted a doughnut he was told, "I can do the ten push-ups myself."

The professor explained that only JD could do the push-ups. Nate responded, "In that case I don't want a doughnut."

But the professor turned to JD and asked him to do the ten push-ups anyway, so that Nate could have access to a doughnut he did not want. JD did the push-ups and Nate became angry: "I didn't want a doughnut and I don't need anybody doing push-ups for me!"

The professor replied, "This is my class and these are my doughnuts. If you don't want one, just leave it on the desk."

He continued on to each student's desk and asked the same question again and again. Regardless of their response, JD would do ten push-ups for each student and a doughnut would be deposited on each desk. By the time the professor got to the last row, JD was sweating and straining to complete each set of push-ups. Then a student passing by stuck his head in the door to enquire about the strange activity in the classroom and the professor invited him in, offering him a doughnut. JD slowly did ten push-ups for the newcomer.

Sitting on the back row, Danielle could bear the spectacle no longer. "You're hurting him!" she said to the professor, pointing to JD's obvious distress. "Won't you at least let someone else do the push-ups?"

The professor replied, "No, JD must do it all alone. I have given him the task to see that everyone present has the opportunity to have a doughnut whether they want it or not. Since JD is the only student with a perfect grade in my class and it's my party, the rule is that only JD can pay the price by doing each of your push-ups."

The professor paused and looked around the classroom before continuing: "Now that I have your full attention I'm sure the analogy here is not too hard to follow. Jesus Christ, the only perfect human, obeyed God, The Father, and died on the cross for each of us so that we could receive the gift of eternal life. Like some of you, there are people who will not accept this free gift, but whether or not you take it, the price has been paid. Jesus did this because He loves us. How will you respond to that love?"

Jonathan Leber was motivated by his personal experience of the love of Christ to dedicate his life to preaching the gospel. In his brief time on earth he shared the precious story many times, weaving it into sermons and testimonies and one-on-one encounters with unbelievers and skeptics. Here is his simple outline of God's salvation plan.

THE BEAUTY OF SALVATION
John 3:16:

For God so loved the world that He gave His only begotten Son that whosoever believeth in Him shall not perish but have everlasting life.

The Apostle Paul explained in his letter to the Ephesians that salvation does not come by our works but by an act of God. Jesus died for each of us so that we might have the opportunity to receive that blessed gift of salvation and spend eternity with Him in Heaven. To accept Jesus into your heart, there are three things that you must know and one simple thing that you must do.

I. **Realize You Are a Sinner-Romans 3:23.**
    For all have sinned and come short of the glory of God.
    We are all sinners, and therefore we come short of the blessings which God has for us. If all of us were lined up on the coast of California, ready to compete in a swim to Hawaii, do you think you'd make it? I know I wouldn't. We all would come short of that goal. In the same way we are all sinners who fall short of God's perfect standard, and therefore we do not have a relationship with God.

II. **Realize the Consequences of Sin-6:23a.**
    For the wages of sin is death...

The penalty for sin is death. Not physical death, but spiritual death. This death is an eternity in Hell. If you die today or Christ comes back, and you do not know Him as your Savior, you will spend eternity in Hell.

III. **Realize the Great Gift-Romans 6:23b**
...but the gift of God is eternal life through Jesus Christ our Lord.
Christ has a gift that He wants to give you. It is a great gift of Salvation that comes only from God, who sent His Son, Jesus, to die on the cross for us all.

IV. **How to Accept the Great Gift-Romans 10:9.**
If thou shalt confess with thy mouth the Lord Jesus, and shalt believe in thine heart that God hath raised him from the dead, thou shalt be saved.
All you need to do to receive this great gift is to ask Christ to forgive you of your sins and believe in your heart that He conquered death by rising from the dead. On the basis of what He has done, and your response to it, you will be saved.
Romans 10:13:
For whosoever shall call upon the name of the Lord shall be saved.'

Is God real to you? The God who was real to Jonathan in this life is still real to him today. The words to the song *My Christ is Real to Me* by Lois R. Irwin express this reality:

> There was a time when Jesus, was just a story told; I spoke about His birthplace, within a manger's fold.
> I sang about His sufferings upon a rugged tree;
> But in my heart I wondered if this could really be.

> I found one day I could not go one step farther on
> Then I remembered Jesus, my hope was not quite gone.
> I cried, Oh Lord, forgive me, help Thou my unbelief,
> If you are real and love me, please bring me sweet relief.

> But now my Christ is real to me, He's as real as real can be.
> He opened up my eyes, and now praise God I see;
> My life that was so empty, He filled with victory,
> And Glory Hallelujah, My Christ is real to me.

Please consider making God real in your life. Everyone is a sinner. What makes a difference is that a believer in Christ is a sinner saved by the grace of God!

YOU CAN GO TO HEAVEN
Without Health,
  Without Wealth,
    Without Fame,
      Without a Great Name,
        Without Learning,
          Without Big Earning,
            Without Culture,
              Without Beauty,
                Without Friends,
                  Without Ten Thousand Other Things
BUT YOU CAN NEVER GO TO
HEAVEN WITHOUT CHRIST!

Epilogue: A Letter To "Ace" April 29, 2006

Dear Ace,

It's been just over a year since you left us. A lot has changed since then; I've changed since then, but then you probably know all of that. Your accident blind-sided me and those closest to you. One day you were the Ace that we all loved hanging out with, but the next day you were a memory—not even a body in a casket we could say goodbye to, just pictures and memories. That is hard, bro. I know that you probably don't have any desire to be back here dealing with life again, but you left a massive hole when you took off—a hole that has not been easy to fill. Maybe the pain is really just me being a little jealous that you're already finished with this life and that your new life is free from sin and struggle, and I'm still here dealing with all of those things;

maybe part of the pain is realizing that you don't miss me because you are in a far, far better place!

Dude, these things have been really hard for me to come to grips with. Time has only helped in the sense that I'm getting used to the hole being there, but your absence still really hurts...

I'll never forget that horrible Tuesday morning-it should have been fun, it was the last day of classes and my graduation was only a week and a half away. Instead I had all sorts of reporters asking me to sum up my friendship with you and try to explain to them what kind of guy you were (that's the only time in my life I've made the front page). It wasn't really fair—I was so numb from the news that everything I said was mechanical. I hope I didn't misrepresent you; but I did want people to know who you were. All the while I was trying to wrap my mind around the fact that my friendship with you was all just memories now. That's a lot to swallow in the space of four hours.

I had all sorts of people ask "how are you?" and they meant well, but it is such a trite question after something like that. I'm still in shock so I can't even tell people how I am. Instead I give the patented answer of "I've been better" or "I'm hanging in there" or some other cliché. My heart was touched by the expressions of care and concern that people were showing, but I couldn't really bring myself to share all of what I was going through with them—good grief, I wasn't even sure what I felt! One second it was deep pain, then the next anger, then sorrow and on and on it went. In a sense I felt as if I was betraying my Christianity to voice doubts and fears and burdens; because for as long as I can remember it has been drilled into me that "God makes no mistakes" and "His will is always perfect" and "He knows what is best" and of course these are all true but none of it helped me deal with the pain. So as a result of not wanting to betray my cultural Christianity and not wanting to unload on someone who could not know what I was going through, the burden of your loss was dealt with for the most part privately. I know this would have disappointed you—you would have wanted me to be confident, to have me be fine with your "flight home." It just wasn't that easy for me though: the pain was too great to just ignore. Maybe I should have talked this all out sooner with someone, but it just felt wrong to my Christianity to dump all this junk that I was dealing with on somebody; especially when I was the one who was supposed to be strong. I wasn't dumb enough to blame God, but it didn't seem like there was any way to deal with the pain.

My mind was continually wandering around the fields of memory. It seemed like I could remember every conversation we had in precise detail. I could remember every time we did stuff together and where we did it and what we ate and who was with us. Times and places that I didn't even know I remembered came flooding back to me after you left.

I never once thought that of all my friends you would be the one to leave us young—you were Ace! You were in better shape than I ever hope to be in. You were so confident. You had so many connections. I've never met anyone else who knew as many people as you did. It seemed like your life was so planned out. If there was anyone who could have done whatever they wanted with themselves it would have been you. This was the Ace that I knew; I just always expected that you would be around for years and years, and that we would be friends for the rest of a long life, but then you left and I was reminded that I can't presume anything.

I told you things are different now; I told you I was different. In a lot of ways it all started with you dying, but I think you would like how I've grown and changed. I think this was one of the few times in my life where I exercised real faith. I wanted to quit, I wanted to believe that the pain would go, I wanted it all to end. But I made a conscious decision that just because I couldn't see a reason or just because it hurt so bad didn't mean that I was going to stop believing that God is. My faith is so much stronger now and my relationship with God has deepened and blossomed in ways that I wasn't sure were possible. Life has taken on a much more serious outlook for me. There isn't a day that goes by where I don't remember you and remembering you reminds me that I only have so long to live. My final days need to be marked with a love for God that consumes my love for others. It's ironic for me to say this, but your death had more impact on me than your life did—maybe that is what you would have wanted. You always wanted to touch people's lives, and when you were alive you did, but when you died you grabbed hold of people's lives and shook them up.

I really miss you bro, especially at this time of the year when it all happened. You would have been graduating next week. But you're not sad about missing that, are you? You're not at all sad about having your life cut short. I wish I could have your perspective right now because it's not clouded by sin and personal sorrow, and your faith has finally been made sight. Even though my faith is still blind, I rejoice that I have a confident hope that someday I will join you again.

I probably won't write you another letter before that time I see you—I don't think I need to, but I did want to tell you that it still is hard, but that I've grown so much because of all of it.

I hope you don't mind but I'm going to put this letter on my blog; because I know that a lot of other people have gone through something similar to this, and if they haven't yet, they will, because this is life. I know you would want me to be honest about dealing with your absence and that you would hope that other people would be able to learn from my honesty. For the first time, then, I'm going to put what I went through in a place where lots of people can read and learn from it all. There you go, touching me from the grave again!

I will always miss you but I'm eternally grateful for how you changed my life.

—Matty Ledgerwood.

Printed in the United States
65722LVS00001B/1-99